In Wisdom
Thou Hast Made Them

Sister Ruth greets her first students

In Wisdom
Thou Hast Made Them

The Reverend Mother Ruth, C.H.S.

Adams, Bannister, Cox
New York

Adams, Bannister, Cox
460 Riverside Drive, New York, 10027
Copyright © 1986 The Reverend Mother Ruth, C.H.S.

All photographs are from the archives of the
Community of the Holy Spirit

Book design by Three Sisters Graphics

Library of Congress Cataloging-in-Publication Data
Ruth, Reverend Mother, C.H.S., 1897-
In wisdom thou hast made them.
1. Community of the Holy Spirit (New York, N.Y.)—
History. I. Title.
BX5973.C66R88 1986   271'.98   86-26491

Printed in the United States of America
ISBN: 0-937431-01-X

Contents

Foreword

Reading this compact book, which will commend itself in the process, is like being received at the Convent of the Holy Spirit in West 113th Street in Manhattan, for tea and conversation with Mother Ruth, or passing among youthful energetic students to say prayers in the Chapel of St. Hilda's and St. Hugh's School nearby, or looking out a window of St. Cuthbert's Retreat House, Melrose. You are apt to get the feeling: there's more here than meets the eye.

This book is an offering about an offering, neither of which is complete nor exhaustive, but happily, hopefully, lovingly and faithfully continuing and refreshing. It is, if you please and have never met Mother Ruth or the Sisters of the Community of the Holy Spirit, an introduction to living examples of faith, hope and love incarnate and in action.

This group of Christian women in the Anglican-Episcopal tradition, having been moved in faith and love voluntarily to live in community under the vows of poverty, chastity and obedience, and dedicated to offering education in the Christian spirit to any they can serve have learned confidence in their mission through shared "prayer and silence, friendship and laughter, love and listening." As noted in this record, when faced with the tremendous task of securing a new adequate building for St. Hilda's and St. Hugh's School in New York, they said: "We Sisters had certainties about this building being God's plan, and in spite of apparent insurmountable obstacles we felt we would finally be able to achieve our purpose." And they did and do. They understand that the power behind their work is, of course, that which emanates from the spiritual lives of the community. The power is understated and immeasurable. Their service is faithfully offered without requiring recognition, believing that sharing the true means of the good life is pleasing to God and that pleasing God is the true means of the good life.

Mother Ruth and the Sisters did not think a book about themselves necessary to their offering. This book is a product of obedience in response to the urging and requests of two bishops who have served and appreciate the Community of the Holy Spirit and Mother Ruth. That appreciation included awareness of the need for a written first-hand account of the Community's origin, purpose and experience from the Community's first person. The introduction gained in reading this account will quicken and increase other's appreciation and awareness of talented pens in the Church's larger community to continue the biographical history of this Community of the Holy Spirit and other such communities of consecration and conservation within the Church's life wherein service for others is the daily offering. There is more here than meets the eye.

John M. Allin
23rd Presiding Bishop
The Episcopal Church

Preface

It gives me great and particular pleasure to commend this straightforward and unassuming account of two remarkable events of recent times, for the common good and in the city and Diocese of New York: the founding of two Christian Schools and of a new Religious Community.

It is altogether fitting and salutary that this record should be presented to us by Mother Ruth, the inspiration and founder of both enterprises.

Since the beginning, now some thirty-seven years ago, I have had the joy and privilege of serving as Chairman of the Board of Trustees of both St. Hilda's and St. Hugh's and the Melrose Schools, and as the Episcopal Visitor to the Community of the Holy Spirit.

Many friends and interested persons, some with great generosity of time and talents and substance, have made their valued and lasting contributions to the life and work, even the continued existence of the schools.   But without the genius, the faith, the total dedication and the tireless labors of Mother Ruth and the religious community which came into being, first in the heart and mind and soul of the Mother Foundress, when with Sister Edith Margaret, she first came to New York so long ago, there would have been no schools at all, nor could they continue into the future as unique centers of Christian light and life and learning.

Horace W. B. Donegan
XII Bishop of New York

Acknowledgments

In the autumn of 1984, Bishop John M. Allin, the twenty-third Presiding Bishop of the Episcopal Church, together with Bishop Horace W. B. Donegan, Visitor of the Community of the Holy Spirit from its beginnings, urged me to record the history of the Community, its life and its works. This is the last thing I would have chosen to do; it could not have been done without the help of a number of people. I am especially grateful to Bishop Allin, who has continued his support throughout.

This record could not have been written without the help of my Sisters. Especially I am grateful to Sister Mary Monica and Mother Elise who have told the story of the Melrose School and Convent; to Sister Lucia for her descriptions of St. Cuthbert's Retreat House and the growth and development of the Associates' program; and to Sisters Virginia Mary, Penelope Mary and Josephine for putting together our memories of converting the three buildings on 113th Street from School to City Convent.

Let me also express my gratitude to the Reverend Ernest "Corky" Miller, alumnus, to Lorca Morello, alumna, and to George Wolf, sometime faculty member of St. Hilda's and St. Hugh's School—valued friends—for their support encouragement and suggestions.

Above all, my profound gratitude is due with pleasure to Shirlie Verrill Harrison, cherished faculty member for nineteen years, who was asked to be the first and chief Reader and who has given very much time in careful, imaginative, loving, discerning consideration of the details of this writing.

The Reverend Mother Ruth, C.H.S.

I

Beginnings

In the spring of 1985 a request came to Mother Ruth, C.H.S., from two bishops in New York, Bishop Donegan and Bishop Allin, for the story in writing of St. Hilda's and St. Hugh's School on Morningside Heights and the Melrose School near Brewster, New York. The bishops requested as well a brief biographical sketch of the founding Sisters of these Schools with a word about any fundamental changes in the Religious life they represented.

Literally thousands of boys and girls have passed through these schools in more than thirty-five years. The majority are now grown up and a number are sending their children to these schools. Many of their graduates are making a considerable contribution to life in various other parts of the world as well as in America. There are also more than one thousand men and women who are associated with the Sisters and their work and who have a continuous prayer link with The Community of the Holy Spirit, which is the creative spiritual energy upon which all the rest depends. The memories which follow have to do not only with the Sisters, who are the chief actors in this drama, but also with the many other people who are connected in some essential way with it all.

The two people whom the Holy Spirit of God chose to use from the beginning for His new work in New York were surprised and all but incredulous. They were Ruth Younger of New York City and Edith Brown of Buffalo, New York.

Edith Brown lived through a good and happy time of growing up with her parents and two brothers. She was a devout child who cared about reading her Bible, praying and attending Sunday School. Her whole family was interested in the poor and needy and did whatever they could to help them. In due course she was confirmed by Bishop Brent, the bishop of her diocese. With a growing sense of Religious Vocation and since Toronto and the Sisters of St. John the Divine were not too far from her home, she visited that Community with fair frequency at the weekends when she was free from her office work. In due course she applied to enter the Novitiate in Toronto and was accepted for training in the Sisterhood of St. John the Divine, where she finally made her vows.

Sister's work in the Community was always well done. She was first taught to do special work in what was known as the "Embroidery Room," where fine hand sewing was required on silk embroidered vestments which the Mother Foundress Hannah had done for many years both for her Convent and for churches in the diocese and elsewhere. Sister Edith Margaret's next assignment was the Altar Bread Department, where she undertook all aspects of preparation of the wafers for Holy Communion as well as the completion and sending of orders wherever required by churches and altars in other places where Holy Communion was celebrated. Both of these appointments were of considerable duration. The major advantage that Sister had in most of her work as well as in her study as a Novice was the opportunity to listen for and to hear the "word of the Lord"—an unusual advantage for anyone who is seeking to understand the life of the Spirit of God. Her lengthy appointment in accounting and in being Treasurer did not disturb the quiet inner life she continued to develop.

Ruth Younger was born in New York City where her parents and siblings lived. She also had good and devout parents who attended the Presbyterian Church. Bible reading and praying together was the norm of her family life. A long period of serious illness meant months in St. Luke's Hospital and subsequently a recuperative time in Virginia. A year later she was able to return to New York to her family and to attend school again. Her Baptism and Confirmation at St. Philip's Church made a very deep impression upon her so that she became a young woman of prayer and almost daily attendance at Mass, even though she was very busy with high school work. Presently she attended one of the chapels in the Cathedral of St. John the Divine and worshipped with the Deaconesses in training, though they did not come to know each other personally. In her spare time she learned church embroidery from Harriet Bronson of St. Hilda Guild. This was a very attractive occupation as was also the happy friendship with Miss Bronson, who daily attended St. Luke's Chapel, Hudson Street in Greenwich Village, New York. The friendship between the two, far apart though they were in age and background, grew so that confidences were exchanged.

Miss Bronson was an Associate of St. Mary's Convent, Peekskill, and Ruth Younger a member of the Confraternity of the Love of God of the Holy Cross Monastery in the city. In due course, each of them considered the possibility of membership in the Conventual Life. Both applications were turned down, however. Miss Bronson was considered less physically strong than such a life demanded of its members, and Ruth Younger's application was rejected because of a strain of "other blood," which was an unacceptable accommodation at that time to southern members of St. Mary's Community. Thereupon Father Hughson, O.H.C., made a successful application for her to leave her country and test her vocation in Canada in the Sisterhood of St. John the Divine (S.S.J.D.). She was very uncertain about this unimagined change, but she was finally willing to try, even though the price seemed at that time all but overwhelming.

Mother Dora received her as a new Postulant into the Community before she was twenty-one and during the First World War. The Sacramental life of prayer, Communion, meditation, and the divine office were familiar. What had to be learned was how to live with and thereby grow from the Sacramental life. There were many opportunities for kindnesses and thought for these new people, who took some time to get to know her because of the practice of much silence. How blessed, really, for it threw her, the new stranger, back upon God and removed selfseeking. Learning to pray in reality made the difference.

Since many new kinds of work were given to most of the Novices in the Novitiate during these war years, it was not unusual for Sister Ruth, who had been Clothed as a Novice, to be told to assist in the Sisters' Hospital pharmacy because of her knowledge of and interest in chemistry. Several Sisters who might have helped in the pharmacy were in the process of nurse's training at this time when the need for trained and experienced personnel was incalculable. The English South African chemist who was there for "the duration" permitted Sister Ruth to assist her more than she thought possible, since Sister's work pleased her. She finally asked Sister to return with her to South Africa. Mother Dora, when approached, agreed with Sister Ruth that she was not able to leave her Novitiate training, even though the work in South Africa had a sense of "call." Mother Dora made this first "temptation" less difficult by being willing for Sister Ruth to go to college in Toronto when she was further along in her novitiate training.

After graduating from St. Hilda's College, Trinity University, she was able to take a graduate course in education at the College of Education in Toronto after her Profession as a Sister on December 29, 1922. She had but a short time in professional teaching, however, because of the pressing need for work in accounting and especially with children in the slums. The aftermath of war and the general depression in Canada and in America were difficult to deal with in a spirit of love, hope, and certainty that "all would be well."

Sister's next assignment was to the Mission House in Montreal, where three priests were in attendance in the large parish church of St. John the Evangelist. The Sisters from the Mission House in the slums visited, taught and served with very loving concern the poor families that lived near the mission.

Not only in Montreal and New York, however, was there work of Sisters of the kind and quality that Mary Simkhovitch speaks of in her book, *Neighborhood: My Story of Greenwich House* (W. W. Norton, New York, 1938). In her own work and in the other American volumes she cites, Mrs. Simkhovitch makes it clear that all of us everywhere who know God and desire to follow, serve, and love Him must give loving service to those whose lot is in any sense cast with ours. Mrs. Simkhovitch's work greatly influenced Sister Ruth's formative thinking.

The assignment which followed the Mission House in Montreal was to St. Cyprian's black church in Detroit, Michigan, not far from the motor car industry. Father Dade, the rector, had sent a request to the Toronto Community to send one Sister to assist him and his people in their church work and their religious parish life, but living space was a problem. One of the parish families living at a distance from the church was uncertain when asked whether they could take in a Sister, because of inadequate room and especially because they wished their little house for themselves at the end of the work and school day. Presently a change was made in the Sister's living quarters near the church, but to the disadvantage of another family with children. The Sister could live there but the family must find another place to live! The Sister was left to live alone, and tried hard to find out what was actually desired and possible in these circumstances. She made the effort to do any really helpful and useful and constructive mission work. Nevertheless, it was all most difficult. Fortunately the children were friendly, responsive and loving, and could be taught. Certainly they were poor and needed as much help as possible with their education. However, the Sister was uncertain about this total situation.

Again Mary Simkhovitch, who had developed successful social work at Greenwich House in the "Village" in New York came frequently to mind as a guide and beacon. It seemed to Sister, after careful consideration and prayer, that she ought to ask her Canadian Community for leave to go back to New York where vision and guidance and essential help would be available in social work if that was what she ought to be doing. Since the Constitution of S.S.J.D. in Toronto provided for such a transfer, the Community then went through the necessary meetings. At one of these meetings the Bishop of Niagara, Bishop Broughall, the Episcopal Visitor of S.S.J.D., was present with the Sisters and the Reverend Mother and a leave of absence was discussed and finally settled. The Bishop's words to Sister Ruth were:

"I send you forth as Abraham
with my blessing to do God's work
wherever He may call you."

He then obtained the Sisters' blessing and thus the new "trial run" was to begin. However, the Rector of St. Thomas' Church, Toronto, Father Stuart, was sure that Sister Ruth should not be sent to do new work alone. Sister Edith Margaret, hearing of this, volunteered at once to set out for the unknown with Sister Ruth. Each Sister was presently given copies of the formal leave of absence and instructions to wear the S.S.J.D. habit. By God's grace Sister Edith Margaret made the whole adventure possible and workable and gave her "all" to it under the Holy Spirit's guidance. Courage, trust, and the most complete givingness to the new call were needed and provided by the Holy Spirit of God to these two Sisters. It was their utter dependence upon Him from the very beginning that enabled them to receive the love and loyalty and understanding of the many hundreds of people whom they were to encounter during the years that followed.

II

New York

Sister Ruth and Sister Edith Margaret soon left for New York and were guests for a brief time at Trinity Mission House in Greenwich Village, which was under the care of the Sisters of St. Margaret. They then boarded ship and sailed for England, their purpose being to learn more about the life and work of the various religious orders that they might understand more fully the actual living under vows and working more completely for God and their neighbors.

It was March 1949. England was still suffering from the disruptions of the war years. There were many children whose parents were still far away in all parts of the world. Sister

Edith Margaret took a course for the training of children in
religion at St. Christopher's College, Blackheath. Sister Ruth
stayed with a friend who had a boarding school for very little
children at Rottingdean on the South Sea Coast while their
parents were away. There she learned a great deal about the
daily life of the very little child and the place of the adult in it.

Among the Religious Communities Sister Ruth visited at this
time were the Community of St. Mary the Virgin at Wantage,
St. Peter's, Woking, St. John Baptist at Clewer, the Community of St. Denys, and St. Margaret's. A number of Communities were visited subsequently from which a rich addition
was also obtained. There was much to learn, particularly
about the corporate spiritual life, the sense of family life, and
the private prayer life. The special work done by each Community was a lesson in many ways, but the most important
truth that both Sisters took away was what they already knew
in part: "I belong to God" and "I belong in love to all my
Sisters and to everyone whom I can serve in any way."

Bishop Donegan was visiting a Midlands church on one of
the Sundays on which Sister Ruth was present and heard him
preach. Meeting her after the service, he was kindness itself
and was interested and attentive to what she could tell him
about the two Sisters' possible future in New York, though
there was but little opportunity to do so at this first meeting.

Sister Ruth had been told at the Church House in
Westminster when she asked about possible interest in the proposed work in New York to "go and see Eddie West. He will
help you. If he isn't in New York when you return, write to
him and he will help all he can." One additional visit Sister
Ruth desired to make before both Sisters returned to New
York was to Whitby, Yorkshire, St. Hilda's well known part
of England. Having graduated from the Toronto College
named for St. Hilda, she wanted very much to see this Chapel

in York Minster. The following letter remembering this visit was sent to Sister Ruth much later by Kathleen Stewart-Smith, who with her husband and mother lived on the Close at this time:

"Our first meeting with Sister Ruth as we knew her then was in 1949. At that time she was given leave by her Toronto Community, the Sisters of St. John the Divine, having all the necessary permissions from that Community and having permission from the Bishop of New York to found a new work there—possibly a Community and a School. She was visiting Schools and Convents in England simply observing and learning all she could.

"Our introduction came from the Prioress of Whitby, Mother Margaret of the Order of the Holy Paraclete, who asked my husband to show a Sister from the U.S.A. around York Minster. He at that time was a Vicar Choral.

"What a delight this almost chance meeting proved to be, and what a wealth of joy and inspiration throughout the remainder of our lives.

"Sister was shown the Minster and all its glories of architecture, stained glass, plate and treasures and she attended Evensong sung in full choir. We took her home for tea and by then the friendship was sealed. She stayed for supper and into the night. I put a breakfast tray in her room and at 3 AM we saw her leaving for York Station and for Oxford where she was due that morning. This incident was wholly typical of the future Mother Ruth and was the characteristic which has attracted us ever since:

Make use of every opportunity.

Never waste time.

Keep real friendships throughout your life."

Sister Edith Margaret and Sister Ruth returned to New York in the middle of August 1949, and rented rooms on Morningside Heights to be near the Cathedral which Sister Ruth had known over the years. They arrived in this unique neighborhood in Upper Manhattan at a time when there were many new building plans. The first of these was a series of "high-rises" built in two or more sections each. The buildings of lower rental are north; the others charge a much higher rent. These houses have been a Godsend, though the racial problems have brought dissatisfactions. The Sisters in their ignorance wished with all their hearts that the neighborhoods near Columbia University might have more basic homogeny, but they gradually became aware of complex reasons why this "ideal" could not work. In any event there was much improvement in places to live, in the hospital situations, and in a considerable number of university advancements. They were grateful.

One of the chief reasons for coming to New York, as was indicated earlier, was that Sister Ruth had been deeply influenced by the books that Mary Simkhovitch had written about her life's work and especially about that part of it having to do with newly arrived immigrant children. She had founded Greenwich House, a Christian center for these people, many of whom were students of the arts and music and other creative works, to come and live and develop their gifts. Mrs. Simkhovitch was a devout woman and by her very example upheld the whole project in a remarkably spiritual way. The Sisters had hoped that they could learn from her how to start and to develop such a settlement house but, alas, they found that she was very ill. Her death came before they had the privilege and opportunity of meeting her personally. However, her husband, a professor of history at Columbia University, came to see Sister Ruth. They had a long talk about the problems involved in putting these kinds of inspirations and ideas into practice, particularly the problems brought about by racial mixtures and international backgrounds. Sister tried to remember at every stage of this experience in her life that "man proposes but God disposes."

Even though they had very little money, they were not fazed. Bishop Manning, the retired former bishop of New York whom Sister Ruth visited, gave her a list of names from the Social Register of people who might be interested. She got in touch with them, many of whom were very distinguished and well known, but understandably they had other things on their minds and felt that they could not take on additional interests.

Again Sister remembered that she had been told in London that the person she must see in New York was "Eddie West," and that he would help them. Since they went to the Cathedral every morning for the early Eucharist, they managed to meet Canon West and to make an appointment with him to introduce him to their story and their need for fulfilling their purpose in New York. His secretary, Miss Kat, made them welcome at once, as did his very friendly Irish setter. Canon West's interest and concern were heartwarming, even though he knew little—if anything at all—about these Sisters except through the credentials they brought. This was the most important moment of the Sisters' lives on the human side since they had left England!

They came to meet several other members of the Cathedral staff, including Canon Green—at that time Headmaster of the resident Choir School—and his wife and their three children. Their introduction to Dr. Wilkie, who worked in pediatrics at St. Luke's Hospital, was also of very considerable importance to them since he had recently returned from the war with the firm decision to do all he could to eliminate war. He was interested in finding a place to begin a school for little children, work for which both Sisters were now eager and ready. The considerable growth of families on Morningside Heights, a not uncommon post-war phenomenon, meant that there were numbers of little children needing at least part-time schooling without delay. And Mr. William Bloor, the Sisters' first Columbia University friend, who was then engaged in preparing a college students' house on 113th Street, was ready and willing to show them how it could be done! Dr. Wilkie and a group of local people he collected round him went to see one of the brownstone houses on 113th Street, viz. 621, and returned with real interest in immediately obtaining and finally purchasing it. The small informal committee was very good to the Sisters and made the brownstone at number 621 available

St. Hilda's House, 621 West 113th Street, New York

without further delay on a lease-hold basis. It was now well into the autumn of 1949. If the School was to open early in 1950, these Sisters must become active in several directions without delay:

1. A group of thoroughly interested parents was the first essential need.

2. Many renovations were necessary to transform this doctor's home and office into a school for little children and a residence for the Sisters. With amazing generosity, ability, and insight it became possible for this small committee to transform the two or three upper floors into a Convent for the Sisters. The first active work on the upper three floors would be reserved for a Chapel, their first requirement, with the final need for Convent rooms set apart in the remaining space.

3. The School itself needed all the space from the entrance to the third floor and it had to be repainted and newly furnished. The "back yard" of the house had to be made into an outdoor play space for little children and baby lavatories installed in suitable places in the School. The entire building soon began to take on suitability even to the possibility of cooking and refrigeration on the second floor rear.

Since Sister Ruth had already made friends with some graduate students at Teacher's College, Columbia University, a group of them came to the school to tell the Sisters about playroom furnishings and appurtenances for kindergarten use, such as a metal and wood sandbox of useful and even large size (similar to the one at Teacher's College), shelves and cupboards all suitably furnished with toys for each sex, paint easels, and much running space both outside in the yard and within the building. After instituting these ideas, they thought themselves possibly ready to show off the beginning of the School after a Christmas party which included refreshments, a movie, and a Christmas tree.

Sister Ruth and Sister Edith Margaret with some of the earliest children in the Spring of 1950

Actually, eight young children were registered by their parents and arrived on the second of February, 1950, the opening day of the new school. By that time there were also four members of the "teaching" group and an Indian lady in her attractive sari with long braided hair. She seemed strange to the children, but of real interest nevertheless. The Sisters were happy to have her there with her little girl as a member of the kindergarten, for they were determined that from the beginning suitable children of all origins must be welcomed.

The Sisters' living accommodations being in the same building as the School was, if anything, an asset. The Chapel on the third floor was in frequent use at once; indeed Canon West celebrated Holy Communion for the Sisters there as soon as there was the essential altar and other necessary appurtenances. Since this first session of the School was really only a half-day arrangement, it was possible to settle many things that afforded the establishment a sense of stability and "settling in"

well before June came. One of the touching daily experiences
that the faculty members enjoyed was being ready at the front
door to meet the children as they arrived with their expectant
and often gleeful little faces. One of them, Canon Green's
seventeen-month-old daughter, was very special. Her mother
brought her to School each morning expecting to disrobe her
and have her "right" for a parting kiss. Not so, indeed! She
would head straight for the playroom where the other children
followed her in everything she did. At nap time when she
spread out her mat, all the
other children did the same
with no further ado. The
program of singing, painting, block building, story
hearing, with a daily
Chapel service of prayer
and "song" grew to mean
more and more to the ma-
jority of the children. The
fieldwork of Teacher's
College students continued
to be a growing asset to
the School. It was all now
well established and the
Sisters were ready, all

Sister Ruth with Billy

things considered, to offer by September Grades I and II as
well as two kindergarten classes.

The next major problem was sufficient room for expansion.
Did the School dare venture to open a second building for
additional classes? After much thought and consultation with
the School's informal group of trustees, it was decided to
secure a second house at number 623 on 113th Street, which
adjoined the first. The School continued to grow by leaps and

bounds, and by 1955 had three adjoining buildings with 190 children from kindergarten through Grade IX.

In addition to directing the School and Convent, Mother Ruth had the pleasure of teaching science and mathematics to the Grade VI class. A boy in her science class was unbelievably fascinated by animals. During class discussions she would find him completely absorbed in a book on one of his favorite wild animals which he tried to keep hidden under his desk. One night a call came from St. Luke's Hospital. It was his mother's voice begging the Sisters' Compline prayers for him. He had fallen out of the window of their apartment building during a pillow fight with his younger brother. With great presence of mind he had caught hold of a spiked fence on the way down and was thus saved from death by this break in his fall. Nevertheless, a spike had driven into his leg. Certainly, prayers were continuous. The Sisters also telephoned a nurse friend, Alida Agor, who went to the hospital at once and found him in very poor shape. When she asked what she could do for him he replied,

"Tell me a story."

"What shall I tell you about, Russell?" she asked.

"Skunks" was the immediate reply.

She was so happy to oblige, and he was so comforted that he dropped off to sleep at last. He spent a year in the hospital. A few years later, the Sisters met him again in Switzerland, bearing a walking cane, but getting ready for high school!

Even with the School's limited resources the Sisters always tried to provide the children with a well-rounded life. On fine days they went to Riverside Park for games, and had dancing and tumbling indoors. Once in a while the entire school would be transformed by a day of fun organized by the parents, faculty, and Sisters. The children put on plays and puppet shows, and some of the parents donated their crafts and skills.

In the spring, an annual benefit concert was held for the scholarship fund wherein the classes competed to see who could sell the most tickets. The progress of the race was illustrated by a large chart in the front hallway of sailboats racing to the finish line or parachuters dropping to the ground or some similar graphic means. In the beginning the concert programs were given by parents who were professional musicians or by an occasional skilled prodigy from the School. Within a few years the gifted music teacher, William Toole, developed a chorus, an orchestra, and other musical groups that performed not only in the School, but they were also invited occasionally to perform in various Churches in the city.

One very important tradition that began almost at the beginning of the life of the School was the Christmas Pageant, which were originally performed in the Chapel of Columbia University but continued very soon after, for want of space, at the Cathedral of St. John the Divine. This was the Christmas story illustrated in mime with narration from the Bible and enriched and reinforced by hymns, carols and canticles. Many of the boys and girls took part—and still do take part—in this cast from the age of a few months (the Infant Jesus) to seventeen-year-old high school students representing old Simeon and Anna in the temple scene. It also means that spontaneously the children and the parents distance themselves from the tinsel and "stuff" of Christmas and grasp the meaning of God becoming man in this very simple, humble way in a stable. For many years the responsibility for the preparation for this Pageant was placed in the gifted and capable hands of Mother Mary Christabel and Shirlie Harrison, whose work will never be forgotten. (see Appendix)

Charterhouse

III

Charterhouse

The Sisters had gone so far as to admit four high school seniors to the last of the three houses which had been purchased on West 113th Street. They were quite serious adolescents who were given to solid academic work, but they were not at the same level in their high school work. The situation in which they found themselves was due in large part to their having to move from homes some distance away. Their schooling became a matter of tutoring in several different subjects. The Sisters thought that they could manage, hoping to succeed in bringing them through to the college entrance level both parents and students desired.

Meantime, however, the Sisters had the excellent good fortune to hear that the Semple School for Girls on Riverside Drive at 107th Street wished to sell its school building and furnishings at once if they could find a purchaser. Could St. Hilda's manage yet a fourth house? What about the distance from the three other houses on 113th Street? The matter was discussed very carefully with members of the School Board, as well as with some of the senior and experienced Sisters and parents. With what was thought to be the most careful consideration in every direction, it was settled to buy the Semple School lock, stock, and barrel. This building, unique inside and out, had previously belonged to a wealthy tobacconist who indeed had built it with special features: a pair of stone lions guarded the main entrance. The rooms were fashioned of a variety of unique and excellent woods. The drawing room was the most rare and humanly gratifying of them all, with its semi-swinging and handpainted gauze ceiling on which were satin angels of many unimaginable colors and activities. There was also a grand mantlepiece of carved stone. Until other arrangements could be made for a Chapel, the Sisters were obliged to worship in this unusual grand room.

Canon West and Mother Ruth discussed the matter and decided to ask the Bishop to allow the use of St. James' Chapel at the Cathedral for the daily middle and high school worship instead of the present drawing room. This meant that the students from Grades VII to XII had to arrive with their teachers in time to begin their daily worship by 8:45. On Thursdays the blessing of a sung Eucharist with organ accompaniment from the small organ loft and a homily from Canon West or Father Guthrie were given. This made for all a beautifully complete and reverent experience which none will ever forget.

A Charterhouse school day begins at the Cathedral

A walk to Charterhouse from morning prayer at the Cathedral

Returning from the Cathedral to Charterhouse meant that out-door games would begin for one level of students at least in the Riverside Park playing field, thus managing out-of-doors sports even in less than desirable weather.

A most immediate need in this schoolhouse, now being used for courses in science and art, was for fire escapes as well as running water on the fourth and fifth floors, needs which were taken in hand as the next priority without delay.

However, the problem about which everyone complained was the lack of adequate heat in zero weather. Even a group of three furnaces did not solve this problem in mid-winter. The School was scheduled for its first inspection by both the Regents from Albany as well as the Middle States Association from Philadelphia. Everyone in Charterhouse as well as St. Hilda's and St. Hugh's tried hard and with much enthusiasm and excitement to be ready for their special visitors. The faculty and students reached the Schools in better than excellent time, but to their utter dismay they found all three furnaces at Charterhouse off duty—a happening with which everyone had to cope! The inspectors donned sweaters and coats, as did students and teachers. The inspectors rose to the occasion as well as everyone else did, and carried on with their work very professionally, hot drinks in many hands. Presently the furnace repair people arrived and all was finally reasonably in hand. Members of the inspecting teams expressed their admiration for the morale of the students and had such very high praise, especially for the mathematics program in senior high school, that one of the inspectors suggested that the math teacher transfer to his high school.

When the School's Trustees received the reports of each of the two agencies that had inspected the four School buildings, it was obviously necessary that careful and wise thinking should take place among them and a decision arrived at that had survival value as its basis. At present the School was indeed the only preschool through twelfth grade co-educational institution on Morningside Heights. Could parents, students, and teachers develop viable certainties for its future?

Some of the Trustees and the Sisters may not have heard of the account written by a parent of three of our students about the place of this School on Morningside Heights. Here is a section of it.

"Morningside Heights in the City of New York is the center of an enormous educational enclave. The primary institution in the area is Columbia University. The collegiate facilities of Morningside Heights include, in addition to the various branches of Columbia University, two major religious seminaries. These, in conjunction with the many churches and synagogues in the community and the presence of the Cathedral Church of St. John the Divine, constitute a far ranging youthful community with spiritual diversity and spiritual values. This religious leavening of the secular majority of our undergraduate institutions makes this community unique in the world.

"The vocational and technical schools listed reveal another facet of the Morningside community. It is the powerful concomitant to the social and cultural applications of our intellectual resources. From law to business to architecture to education to music, our neighborhood vocational schools span the applications of high culture to society.

"Many of these institutions use the propinquity of St. Hilda's and St. Hugh's School to sharpen their own students' skills. This interaction is fostered by the lay and religious teachers in our School, many of whom participate in the opportunities to extend their own competence by using the facilities of the community's other institutions."

The children who made up the student body upon which a number of these parents depended varied considerably. A large number of them came from homes where there was a blend of direction, enthusiasm and support as well as basic religious faith, moral principles that were acted upon, and regard and consideration for each other that make life a full and gratifying experience. But there was also another small group of students who came from the permissive families and homes of the rebellious 1960's, homes which accepted the "youth culture," expected little of honor, truth, or any real moral life, and where personal self-discipline was not the norm, shall we say. However, these boys and girls from childhood through adolescence and young adult life daily associated with those who responded to the requirements of the good life, and some were no doubt helped by this association. The group over which the Sisters agonized constituted the peers who brought into our group life the dangers that are encountered everywhere in schools today. St. Hilda's and St. Hugh's certainly was not exempt from them. The School was, however, looked upon by many as a safe haven for their children in these disruptive times.

The addition of the high school brought with it new and increased student activities, viz., the Student Council, the National Honor Society, College Boards, college preparation, as well as increased personal friendships and very important school dances. Entering the seventh grade classroom one day, it was evident that there was much unhappiness when the members had been excluded from a dance organized by the older grades. This oversight was remedied at once, and a dance for these students was arranged without delay. They transformed their classroom into a dance floor, enthusiastically arranging paper streamers on the walls and pooled their collections of "twist" records. Refreshments were had and opportunities for much talk, laughter, and singing became a ready and easy norm.

All of us adults who had been so absorbed in the School program in its new demands upon us and upon the total School were thus required to remember that all the needs and requirements, and especially the thoughts for the students' priorities, had with the demanding curriculum to become carefully included activities. Certainly, we needed a proper school building with so many legitimate demands provided for and arranged, and this without delay!

IV

The Community

The Community of the Holy Spirit was formally instituted on the 27th of August, 1952. Both Sister Ruth and Sister Edith Margaret knew well the Rule of Life from which they had lately been transferred. Sister Ruth knew also, and valued highly, the Rule of the Oxford Mission to Calcutta, an English missionary order in India. Their Superior, Mother Edith, was happy to have the C.H.S. Sisters use in any way the Rule of the O.M.C. wherever it was an inspiration and support to them. When the new Rule of the Community of the Holy Spirit was ready, a copy was sent to Bishop Donegan in England. That document, along with the Constitution of the new Community, had his approval and would now be used by the new Community as its authority.

During the first year of the School, two new Aspirants were received into the Community with great joy: Sister Catherine, who came from England where she had done extensive mission work, and Sister Elise, who had heard of the Community through the booklets that were allowed to be left in the parish churches around the city. Sister Elise had completed her degree in music at the Juilliard School and had already been accepted by a deaconess training college in Philadelphia. She was actually on the bus en route there to begin her studies when she had an interior conviction which said: "Go and give yourself to God as a Sister." She turned round, cancelled everything, and came to the Community.

The official public recognition and the Church's evidence of the founding of this new Community were treated as part of the Service of Holy Communion, held in St. Ansgar's Chapel of the Cathedral Church of St. John the Divine in New York. Bishop Donegan presided in the chancel; with him was Father Granville Mercer Williams, the Superior of the Society of St. John the Evangelist (S.S.J.E.) and the representative of S.S.J.D. as its Warden. The Reverend Canon Edward N. West was present as the Warden of the new Community. There were also present in the chancel Bishop Boynton and Father Lang. The congregation represented members of other Communities, parents of children, and friends.

While each religious Community in the Church is free to choose its own pattern for the service for the profession of new members, it is always based upon the Community's Rule of Life and its Constitution, and it usually includes the celebration of the Holy Eucharist. In accord with the Church's arrangements for all its liturgies, the Community of the Holy Spirit's Office for the Profession of Sisters is a formal document and is unchanged from that day in August of 1952 when Sister Ruth and Sister Edith Margaret became the new Community's first Sisters.

THE COMMUNITY OF THE HOLY SPIRIT
OFFICE
FOR THE PROFESSION OF SISTERS

The Profession shall be made at the Holy Eucharist. Before the Service, the Girdles, Scapulars, Crosses, Veils and Rings for those who are to be Professed are placed on the Altar.

Introit

Antiphon: Behold the Bridegroom cometh: go ye out to meet Him. Psalm xxvii.

The Lord is my light and my salvation; whom then shall I fear: the Lord is the strength of my life, of whom then shall I be afraid?

One thing have I desired of the Lord, which I will require: even that I may dwell in the house of the Lord all the days of my life, to behold the fair beauty of the Lord, and to visit His temple.

For in the time of trouble He shall hide me in His tabernacle: yea in the secret place of His dwelling shall He hide me, and set me up upon a rock of stone.

Therefore will I offer in His dwelling an oblation with great gladness: I will sing, and speak praises unto the Lord.

My heart hath talked of Thee, seek ye My face: Thy face Lord will I seek.

Antiphon: Behold the Bridegroom cometh: go ye out to meet Him.

The COLLECT

O God, Who hast prepared for them that love Thee such good things as pass man's understanding; pour into our hearts such love towards Thee, that we, loving Thee above all things, may obtain thy promises, which exceed all that we can desire; through Jesus Christ our Lord, Who liveth and reigneth with Thee and the Holy Ghost, ever one God, world without end. Amen.

GRADUAL

God be in my head and in my understanding; God be in my eyes, and in my looking; God be in my mouth, and in my speaking; God be in my heart, and in my thinking; God be at my end, and at my departing.

The GOSPEL   St. Luke xi:9

Jesus said to his disciples, Ask and it shall be given you; seek and ye shall find; knock, and it shall be opened unto you. For everyone that asketh receiveth; and he that seeketh, findeth; and to him that knocketh, it shall be opened. If a son shall ask bread of any of you that is a father, will he give him a stone? Or if he ask a fish, will he for a fish give him a serpent? Or if he shall ask an egg, will he offer him a scorpion? If ye then, being evil, know how to give good gifts unto your children, how much more shall your heavenly Father give the Holy Spirit to them that ask Him?

After the Nicene Creed the Bishop's chair shall be placed before the Altar, the Warden in cope standing on his right hand. The two Sisters who are to renew their Vows, and be transferred into the Community of the Holy Spirit shall stand before the Bishop.

The Bishop: My daughters, what is your desire?

Answer: I desire to bind myself anew to a life of devotion to our Lord Jesus Christ in the Community of the Holy Spirit, under the Vows of Poverty, Chastity, and Obedience.

The Bishop: (To the Warden of the Sisterhood of St. John the Divine) Do you and the Officers and Chapter of the Sisterhood of St. John the Divine, as well as the Episcopal Visitor of that Community, consent that these Sisters shall be transferred to the Community of the Holy Spirit?

The Warden, S.S.J.D.: We do consent.

The Bishop: (To the Sisters) Do you promise to submit to the Rule of the Community of the Holy Spirit, and to observe its customs?

Answer: I do promise, the Lord being my helper.

The Bishop shall then say to each Sister: May God have mercy upon thee and bring thee to his Kingdom. Amen. May the love of God manifest Christ within thee. Amen. May the power of God grant thee the Spirit of meekness. Amen.

The Vow shall then be renewed as follows:

In the Name of God. Amen. I, Sister Ruth/Sister Edith Margaret, inspired by the Holy Spirit of God, and desiring to renew the consecration of myself to Him in body, mind, and spirit, do now renew the Vow of Poverty, the Vow of Chastity, and the Vow of Obedience, which I promise to observe unto my life's end. I desire to undertake these Vows in the Community of the Holy Spirit and under its Rule, steadfastly purposing to keep and observe the same therein forever, the Lord being my helper. And herein I humbly pray for the grace and heavenly assistance of the Holy Spirit through our Lord Jesus Christ. Amen.

The Bishop shall then deliver the Cross to each Sister, saying:

Receive the Cross of our Lord Jesus Christ as a Sister in this Community. In the Name of the Father, and of the Son, and of the Holy Spirit. Amen.

Reception of the Sisters into the Community

The Bishop taking each Sister's right hand shall say:

We receive you, with the full consent and blessing of the Community of your Profession, and admit you into the fellowship of the Community of the Holy Spirit, to be known henceforth as Sister Ruth/Sister Edith Margaret.

God the Father, God the Son, and God the Holy Ghost, bless, preserve, and keep you; the Lord mercifully with his favor look upon you, and bring you to everlasting life. Amen.

The Novices to be Professed shall stand before the Bishop. The Warden shall address the Bishop: Right Reverend Father in God, I present unto you these Novices who desire to make their Profession as Sisters in the Community of the Holy Spirit.

The Bishop: Are you satisfied of their fitness and vocation?

Warden: So far as man's knowledge doth allow, I believe them to be fit and truly called of God to this holy and religious estate.

The Bishop shall then address the Mother-Elect and say: Do you consent that these Novices make their Profession among you?

Mother-Elect: I do so consent.

The Questions

The Bishop: Before admitting you to Profession it is meet that you answer before us and before these witnesses to those things which we in the name of God and his Church shall demand of you:

All present standing up, the following questions are put to the Sisters-Elect:

The Bishop: Do you believe that you are truly called of God to bind yourselves to Him for the rest of your lives in this world?

Answer: I do so believe.

The Bishop: Do you promise to devote yourselves wholly, body, mind and spirit, to God's service forever?

Answer: Relying upon God's infinite grace and mercy, I do so promise.

The Bishop: Have you meditated upon the Rule of this Community, and weighed well the obligation it will impose upon you?

Answer: I have done so.

The Bishop: Do you promise to conform to the Rule of this Community, and to observe its customs?

Answer: I do so promise, the Lord being my helper.

The Bishop: Know this, my daughters, that except the Lord build the house, their labour is but lost that build it; except the Lord keep the city, the watchmen waketh but in vain. Will you then labour only in the Lord, seeking your strength from Him? Will you watch always in the Lord, looking to Him for deliverance to keep your feet from falling? Will you, by constant prayer, seek ever to be guided in your goings and directed in your duties as it shall please the Lord?

Answer: I will do so, by the help of God.

The Bishop:

Our help is in the Name of the Lord.

Who hath made heaven and earth.

The Bishop begins the Veni Creator Spiritus, the Novices devoutly kneeling.

Come, Holy Ghost, our souls inspire,
And lighten with celestial fire;
Thou the anointing Spirit art
Who doest thy sevenfold gifts impart;
Thy blessed unction from above
Is comfort, life and fire of love;
Enable with perpetual light

To dullness of our blinded sight:
Anoint and cheer our soiled face
With the abundance of thy grace:
Keep far our foes, give peace at home:
Where Thou art Guide no ill can come.
Teach us to know the Father, Son,
And Thee, of both, to be but one;
That through the ages all along
This may be our endless song.
Praise to Thy eternal merit,
Father, Son, and Holy Spirit. Amen.

Then shall the Bishop stand and pray over the Sisters Elect:

O God Who didst teach the hearts of Thy faithful people by sending to them the light of thy Holy Spirit; grant to these Thy servants by the same Spirit to have a right judgment in all things and ever more to rejoice in His holy comfort; through the merits of Christ Jesus our Saviour, Who liveth and reigneth with Thee, in the unity of the same Spirit, one God, world without end. Amen.

Formula for making unto God the Three-fold Vow of Poverty, Chastity, and Obedience

The Bishop shall then say (to each Sister-Elect):

May God have mercy upon thee, and bring thee to his Kingdom. Amen. May the love of God manifest Christ within thee. Amen. May the power of God grant thee the Spirit of meekness. Amen.

The Vow shall then be taken as follows:

In the Name of God. Amen. I, _____, inspired by the Holy Spirit of God and willing to consecrate myself to Him forever in body, mind, and spirit, do now make unto

God the Vow of Poverty, the Vow of Chastity, and the Vow of Obedience, which I promise to observe unto my life's end. I desire to undertake these Vows in the Community of the Holy Spirit and under its Rule, steadfastly purposing to keep and observe the same therein forever, the Lord being my helper. And herein I humbly pray for the grace and heavenly assistance of the Holy Spirit, through our Lord Jesus Christ. Amen.

The Bishop shall then say:

Almighty God, who hath given thee this will to do these things; grant also unto thee strength and power to perform the same; through Jesus Christ, our Lord. Amen.

The Bishop shall then deliver the Girdles to each Sister; and the same shall be done with the Scapulars, Veils, Crosses, and Rings, according to the following form:

The Bishop: (At the deliverance of the Girdle) The Lord turn thy heaviness into joy, and gird thee with gladness, that thou mayest give thanks unto him forever.

The Bishop shall then deliver the Scapular to each Sister, saying:

Receive this Scapular in token that thou has taken upon thee the yoke of Christ.

The Bishop shall then deliver the Cross to each Sister, saying: Receive the Cross of our Lord Jesus Christ as a Sister of this Community. In the Name of the Father, and of the Son, and of the Holy Ghost. Amen.

The Bishop shall then deliver the Veil to each Sister, saying:

Receive this Veil, the special symbol of thy entire consecration to Christ, and of the clothing of thy whole being with his love.

The Bishop shall then place the Ring on the fourth finger of each Sister's right hand, saying:

Receive this Ring as the token of perpetual fidelity to him, who is the Bridegroom of the whole Church; may he make thee of the number of those undefiled ones, who follow him wheresoever he goeth, and call thee to the Marriage Supper of the Lamb. In the Name of the Father, and of the Son, and of the Holy Ghost. Amen.

Reception of the Sisters into the Community
The Bishop taking each Sister's right hand shall say:
We receive you, your probation well fulfilled, and admit you

Sister Ruth being made the Reverend
Mother by Bishop Donegan

into the fellowship of the Community of the Holy Spirit, to be known henceforth as Sister _____.

God the Father, God the Son, and God the Holy Ghost bless, preserve and keep you: the Lord mercifully with his favor look upon you, and bring you to everlasting life. Amen.

The newly Professed Sisters shall then return to their places.

The Installation of the Mother
The Warden shall then present to the Bishop the Sister who has been chosen to be the Mother of the Community.

The Warden: Right Reverend Father in God, I present to you this Sister, who has been duly chosen to be Mother of this Community, entreating you to install her with benediction.

The Bishop shall then examine the Mother-Elect in this fashion:

The Bishop: Do you promise to maintain the Rule of this Community?

Answer: I do so promise, the Lord being my helper.

The Bishop: Will you endeavour to give a Mother's love and help to those who are in your care, looking upon this as your chief privilege and duty?

Answer: I will so endeavour, the Lord being my helper.

The Bishop: Do you promise to use the authority committed to you without favour or partiality, striving with equal and open mind to direct the whole power at your disposal to the glory of God?

Answer: I do so promise, the Lord being my helper.

The Reverend Mother Ruth at her blessing by Bishop Donegan when she becomes the Mother of her Sisters

Then shall the Mother-Elect kneel, and the Bishop standing up shall say:

Almighty God, before whom you have made these promises, grant unto you grace and strength to perform the same, that his purposes for this Community may be fulfilled; through Jesus Christ our Lord. Amen.

Take thou authority to rule over this Community and to minister to its members in all things that may promote their welfare, both temporal and spiritual, in the Name of the Father, and of the Son, and of the Holy Ghost. Amen.

We install thee as Mother of the Community of the Holy Spirit, bidding thee to remember the words of our Lord, how he said, He that is greatest among you, let him become as the younger; and he that is chief, as he that doth serve. For verily the Son of Man came not to be ministered unto, but to minister, and to give his life as ransom for many.   Unto

The Reverend Mother Ruth signs the registration book at St. Ansgar's Chapel, the Cathedral

God's gracious mercy and protection we commit thee. The Lord bless thee and keep thee. The Lord make his face to shine upon thee and be gracious unto thee. The Lord lift up the light of his countenance upon thee and give thee peace, both now and evermore. Amen.

The Celebrant shall then proceed with the Order of Holy Communion.

A reception was held in Cathedral House, where many of the clergy, Sisters, parents of the children, and friends met for a time of gratitude that another Episcopalian Community with a School was now available for them and their children. There was much thankfulness throughout on this occasion.

The School Crest on the new School building.

V

St. Hilda's and St. Hugh's

One of the phenomena of the great city of New York is the amazing amount of building that is constantly in progress and is everywhere observable. Already familiar is the kind of building in which the city appears to have the greatest interest: the deluxe model office building erected to replace what appeared but yesterday to be an attractive, useful and well-kept counterpart of an earlier vintage; the numerous housing projects in which tall but colorless and unnecessarily ugly structures replace the more colorful though dilapidated earlier dwelling places; the bizarre and spectacular creations, among them some of the newer museums.

Everywhere there is building in progress. But for us on Morningside Heights, there is development of very considerable and special importance: the housing projects of Morningside Gardens and the Grant Houses have been completed only relatively recently and from them come some children to our School. Riverside Church's new Parish House with a very adequate gymnasium is now in constant use. Barnard's new library and student residence, and Columbia's new Citizenship Building, along with several others but a block away, have been erected with phenomenal speed. The headquarters of the National Council of Churches on Riverside Drive at 120th Street is now in continuous use. Two excellent new wings of St. Luke's Hospital are completed and in use. Other buildings of great importance to Morningside are beyond the planning stage.

Practically all of this building has taken place since one little "Brownstone Front" was bought on West 113th Street in 1950 to house the beginnings of the modern St. Hilda's School. Its very name reminds us that down the ages many other Schools in many parts of the world have been named for this leader in education. The accomplishments of our graduates and our purposes support the persistence of this memory of an unusually great Christian teacher as we ponder her accomplishments and purposes, as well as those of St. Hugh of Charterhouse and Lincoln, whom we have also been willing and grateful to have as namesake and model. Both of these renowned teachers in their different settings and ages were deeply concerned and persistent about the suitable buildings in which they would best be able to make their external contribution to the development of the young lives entrusted to their care.

We had named our Charterhouse on Riverside Drive for St. Hugh with recognition of the historical presence of one

with whom we claimed some kinship. Our first building in
this new Morningside Heights "complex" was named for St.
Hilda with the same prayerful thought. And now came our
decision to build a badly needed larger and more modern
school which would be named for both Saints and would
accommodate more than seven hundred boys and girls from
the time they entered the nursery until their decision about
college was made and they moved on to higher education.

Our need to fulfill our vision of this new School (about
which our Trustees were fully cognizant) had the usual "next
steps" and priorities: a suitable building site, architects'
satisfactory plans, builders' costs, time priorities, and
furnishings. We Sisters had certainties about this building
being God's plan, and in spite of apparent insurmountable
obstacles we felt we would finally be able to achieve our
purpose.

Where to place St. Hilda's and St. Hugh's School on
Morningside Heights? With amazement we came upon an
available site in the next block to our present three brownstone
fronts. Wonderful! (Oh, ye of little faith!)

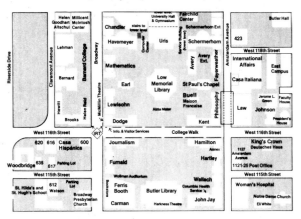

The new building is set in the midst of Columbia University and other
institutions

Architectural drawing of the new school building

Bishop Donegan was well acquainted with the "right" architect, Mr. Robert Hutchins, who was happy to consider plans
for our new School and to find the suitable builder for this
task. However, none of this could be accomplished without
the financial means. We had already a fund-raiser of some
experience who worked as hard as possible to achieve all the
gifts necessary for such a building. He finally applied to
Bishop Donegan for names of those people of means who
might be interested. Among them was Mr. Hermann Place, a
retired vice president of the Chase Bank. Mr. Place, when approached, replied to the request to help with: "Yes, I think I
could be interested in helping to build a new school"—and
interested indeed he proved to be. He worked for eighteen
months to achieve the needed money, and even though it was
eventually gathered largely through loans with the additional
interest, the $4,600,000 was made available; the last payment
to Columbia University being due in January 1988, when the
School will be debt-free.

The approval of plans for our seven-story St. Hilda's and St. Hugh's building was placed in the wise hands of a small experienced committee who, with Bishop Donegan and Mother Ruth, were able to follow the progress of the building, to make the inevitable adjustments, and to open the new School on time, on September 8th, 1967.

En route to the cornerstone laying on a frigid November day

The foundation stone was laid at an unforgettable outdoor service on November 17, 1965, this date appropriately being St. Hilda's and St. Hugh's Day, when there was such bitter cold that the lips of the members of the brass ensemble commissioned to play on this great occasion froze to their instruments. The cornerstone laying began. The foundation stone had been sent to us by the present Mother Prioress of the Holy Paraclete Community at Whitby, and so the Whitby Stone inserted into the large block of Indiana limestone represents "the foundations in tradition, in idealism and in realism upon which the School is built." We include this permanent record from the pen of one of our School boys which appeared in the Charterhouse *Courant* in that current issue.

The cornerstone is laid

Under the Whitby Stone are these words:

"The insert is a stone from St. Hilda's Abbey, Whitby, Yorkshire, England, where this Abbess presided and taught in the 7th Century, A.D."

The President of Columbia University, Dr. Grayson Kirk, placed the memorabilia in its copper box, which was sealed for placement in the cornerstone. Mr. Hermann Place, Vice Chairman of the School Trustees, placed the stone relic in the foundation stone and mortared it in place. He then addressed the Bishop of New York, saying: "Right Reverend Sir, we ask that you bless this foundation stone and lay it to the glory of God." Bishop Donegan then proceeded with the blessing of the foundation stone:

"O Lord Jesus Christ, Son of the living God, who art the brightness of the Father's glory, the express image of his person, the one foundation, and the chief cornerstone: Bless what we do now in laying this stone in thy Name, and be thou, we beseech thee, the beginning, the increase, and the consummation of this work, which is undertaken to the glory of thy Name, who with the Father and the Holy Ghost, livest and reignest, one God, world without end. Amen."

The cornerstone was made ready for laying; the Bishop struck the stone thrice with the trowel and said, "I lay this cornerstone, in the Name of the Father, and of the Son, and of the Holy Ghost. Amen. Except the Lord build the house their labour is but lost that build it; the foundation of God standeth sure, having this seal, the Lord knoweth them that are his."

The cornerstone blessing

And so that very important "first step" being achieved and the large number of guests, parents and students being dispersed, all of us with one accord looked forward eagerly to the School's completion and the entry of the students and teachers into their new School home.

During the interval between the foundation ceremonies of St. Hilda's and St. Hugh's and the actual completion and formal dedication of the School, a large number of details had to be completed which engaged many men and women in their specialties as well as those responsible for professional carpentering, kitchen furnishings, gymnasium setup, lab appointments, lighting facilities, etc. There were, of course, some unforseen difficulties.

The wood with which the Chapel was to be lined had not arrived in time from Wisconsin, for instance. That was indeed one of the most essential parts of the final preparation. Telephoning Wisconsin to inquire about its delivery, we found that it was still in the shed and that it would require days to get it safely to New York! After several further enquiries, we found that it would be "impossible" to get it to the School in time to line the Chapel walls before January's dedication service. And so, the order was given to send all that wood by air freight! Even this plan and the communication it entailed took endless time to accomplish, but finally we had wood for the walls and carpenters to work night and day to place it. And thus it was with so many of the vast number of appurtenances we needed to open our School. Finally, however, with the plumbers' strike over and details complete, and the new School in suitable and reasonable order, we set a date for its dedication: January 12, 1967.

The new school building is dedicated

Over 200 guests were invited to this important occasion, parents, trustees, heads of other Schools, clergy, teachers, students, friends. Bishop Donegan arrived at the School with his Chaplain, Father Terwilliger. Canon West, Father Jones, and Dr. Finch were also in the procession. The Bishop was received at the door of the School by the Reverend Mother, who asked him to dedicate this School. The special dedication service consisted of prayers, hymns, and Holy Scripture, the anthem being read by Sister Edith Margaret. The Bishop, after entering the Chancel, addressed the congregation and dedicated the Chapel and School building. The Te Deum Laudamus was then sung and the prayers for St. Hilda and St. Hugh were said by the Bishop, the service ending with his blessing. A reception followed the service of dedication, with an invitation for all to see the School throughout. Even though, from our point of view, there were many things yet to be done, parents, teachers, and guests who took the opportunity not only to enjoy the party, but actually to review the new School were enthusiastic in their praise.

Mother Ruth receives the Bishop's Cross from Bishop Donegan at the Dedication dinner

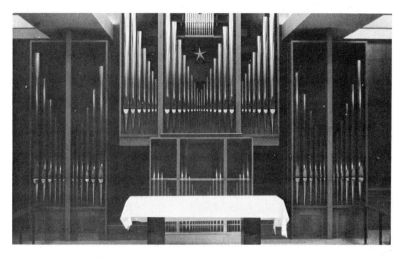

A Reiger organ is installed at the new school

The Yeomen of the Guard

That evening Bishop Donegan arranged a private dinner party in Cathedral House to honor those who had been largely responsible for the School building. Certificates were presented to Mr. Hutchins and Mr. Place, and the Bishop's Cross was given to Mother Ruth with these words:

"Wear this Cross on every important or public occasion, and when you are working late at night, put it on and remember that someone loves you as well as God." Mother Ruth became the first woman in the diocese to receive this Cross, an indication of honor and gratitude reserved for outstanding service to the diocese.

Ten years later, we incorporated a major change into the new building. We were desirous of having an organ in our Chapel and so invited a number of representatives of organ makers to come and review our needs. Mr. William Toole, head of the Music Department, worked hard to obtain the most suitable instrument. After consulting a number of different organ representatives, we decided upon a Reiger organ, and had one made to our use. However, no organ maker could install an instrument to fit the available space in the Chapel unless we were willing to place it in the position of a reredos and build the Sanctuary with its altar in front of it. This necessary accommodation was not, at the time, satisfactory to many of our children, faculty, and parents, nor to many of the Sisters. However, those of us having to make the final choice decided to accept the situation, and after a period of adjustment, most now agree that this location of the organ seems to have preserved the reverence of the dedicated Chapel. All will most certainly agree that the organ itself—one of the finest in the City—has added immeasurable pleasure and beauty to our School services.

Another concomitant major change that it became necessary to make was moving the Chapel seats at right angles to the Sanctuary instead of facing it. This, I understand, has been more satisfactory to the total school family. The Chapel has increasingly been used for other-than-School purposes: the Bishop's special meetings and clergy meetings (with the Holy Eucharist) have been held in our Chapel for some time, with a sense of privilege on our part; weddings, memorial services, and several concerts are part of its short history.

A musical performance at St. Paul's Chapel, Trinity Parish

Other space in our building was also designed for multi-use purposes and has been so used. The gymnasium, for instance, has as part of its structure a stage used not only for theatrical, ballet, and concert presentations, but also for ballet classes during the School day; the gymnasium floor itself is frequently used in the evenings by community groups wanting a place for basketball or volleyball practice or games; it serves also as a rainy day play space for early arriving children. The activities room is a rehearsal and game-playing space as well as an overflow cafeteria at lunchtime. The music room does triple duty as a place for individual instruction and practice in musical instruments or voice, the area for regularly scheduled acting workshops, and the room for chorus and music-theory classes. There is a splendid play-deck open to the skies on the second floor which is used for recess activities by the lower and middle school children and is, too, sometimes used by rehearsing theatre students. The "roof"—a treasured place for Seniors as an unchaperoned privilege reserved only for them—is a perfect sun-bathing spot and is occasionally used in spring and fall by upper-school teachers with their classes.

Mother Mary Christabel with students in the library

None of this top-to-bottom practical and aesthetic use of space by School and community groups has escaped the eyes of accreditation teams. Over the years we have had three very successful accreditations. While they have been demanding of the teachers' and the administration's time and energy, they have helped us to look at ourselves with an outsider's eye and to take stock of our strengths and weaknesses. Much good has come from this self-evaluation.

Science class

Mother Ruth at Animal Show   *Swimming class at Barnard pool*

One aspect of our School that has favorably impressed visiting teams of accreditors is our statement of philosophy and objectives. It shows, they have reported, a school that knows what it is about. While these precepts were worked out on paper by faculty in preparation for accreditation, they have been inherent since our beginnings. They are included here as the principles guiding our work from the time our first little brownstone school opened with eight young children until today when we educate hundreds of children from nursery through Grade XII in a modern, fully equipped building.

The School's Philosophy

We believe that St. Hilda's and St. Hugh's School must consider the three-fold nature of its students—body, mind, and spirit—and must seek to encourage all-round development of the individual as fully as his capacity will allow.

Each student must learn critical and analytical thinking, applying this process of thought to his immediate intellectual pursuits and life experiences. He should endeavor to understand and evaluate his place in society and the world.

The learning experiences of the curriculum are designed to meet the needs of college-directed students who represent the local as well as the mobile populations of America and many parts of the world, and who bring amazing ethnic and cultural diversity to our school. One of the basic duties of St. Hilda's and St. Hugh's School, set in the midst of this exciting and demanding Columbia University neighborhood, is to teach and inspire our students to respond to the unique academic, professional and cultural environment of Morningside Heights.

We believe that, as part of our rigorous curriculum, a thorough program of religious knowledge will help students make right moral choices based upon sound principles of life and a vital faith in God.

Mother Ruth with four graduates

Graduation class with faculty, Canon West, Bishop Donegan, Mother
Ruth, and Columbia University President William McGill

In summary, we believe that our students may expect to leave St. Hilda's and St. Hugh's physically strong, mentally alert, and spiritually equipped to meet the problems and opportunities of their neighborhoods and city as well as those of our troubled but challenging world.

The School's Objectives

In keeping with our philosophy, which focuses on the three-fold nature of children, the following may be considered the ultimate objectives of St. Hilda's and St. Hugh's School:

• To develop sound attitudes and practices in the pursuit of good health, both physical and mental, and to teach respect for the body as an important instrument in which to live a worthy life.

• To develop creativity, and to cultivate aesthetic sensitivity through an understanding of art, drama, music, and dance as means of self-expression and group activity, and to provide opportunities for the discovery and development of individual talent.

• To give our students an understanding of and practice in the fundamental processes of rational and honest thinking, emphasizing a command of basic skills in such areas as language arts and mathematics.

• To prepare a curriculum in the basic disciplines as well as in the newer areas of study, all constantly under review by a carefully chosen curriculum committee.

Graduation with The Rt. Rev. Stephen Bayne, Canon West and Mother Ruth

• To provide for opportunities in and to encourage the practice of responsible citizenship, leadership and cooperation with peers, faculty, and administration of the School in preparation for a life of harmonious interaction and good will.

• To give students direction in their choice of vocation, and guidance in their selection of college, university, or other institution of learning.

• To prepare our students with a thorough knowledge of the Holy Scriptures as the revelation of God to man; and to teach the Judeo-Christian heritage of moral values, and to encourage their application to life, while respecting other religious beliefs and traditions.

• To develop in our students such a sense of the spiritual reality of the world and universe that they are able to obtain a vision of creation as a gift of God for which man must learn to become a responsible steward.

The Board of Trustees (1985)
Standing (L to R) The Reverend Leslie J. A. Lang, Mr. James Riordan,
Professor Eugene Galanter, Mr. William F. Toole, Mr. Peter Iselin,
Bishop Donegan, Mr. Robert S. Hutchins
Seated (L to R) Mrs. David C. Matthew, Mother Ruth, Mrs. James
Armstrong, Mother Elise, Mother Mary Christabel, Sister Mary Monica
(Not present) Mrs. Bromwell Ault, Mr. Joseph Breed, IV, Dr. Matthew
Dann, Mr. John Miles Evans, Dr. Edward R. Finch, Jr., Mr. Nicholas
Gordon, Sister Mary Winifred, Mr. Michael T. Sovern, Canon West

St. Hilda's School becomes the Convent for the Sisters

VI

The Convent

The decision about the separation of St. Hilda's Convent from the school was difficult to make. Should we build two additional stories on the new school, or should we have a separate Convent? Actually the city building code precluded the former choice, and so plans were made for renovating St. Hilda's House (formerly the School) as a Convent for the Sisters.

In June 1966 the Sisters moved out of St. Hilda's House for the reconstruction and joining of the three brownstones into one dwelling—supposedly the work of one summer. The four Sisters who had been sent to Peoria to live in the House of

Studies while attending Bradley University (Sisters Anne, Penelope Mary, Virginia Mary, and Mary Christine) came home to help in this important change in housing.

Sister Virginia Mary recalls, "Our last night at the Convent we labored all night, covered in aprons, dust, and glory, in tagging, organizing, and lugging downstairs every item in the School and Convent, and these seemed to multiply under our fingers. I remember wicker birdcages and garden implements and extra sets of bed springs appearing from nowhere, all to be boxed, labeled, carted, bumped or dragged down the stairs (there was no elevator)."

Sister Penelope Mary remembers, "Yes, and by two in the morning we were all beginning to be filled with merriment. We worked until about four, and had only a short nap before the day's routines began."

The movers came at ten o'clock that morning, taking Community things with red tags to the Cathedral to be stored in the crypt and taking such other things as furnishings and School items with yellow tags to commercial storage. Sisters' choir books and winter clothing were boxed with each Sister's name and a red tag on the outside. Somehow the feat was accomplished and everyone went exhausted but gratefully to her bed in new surroundings.

The Novices were moved to Melrose, the house in Brewster, New York, for the summer. The Sisters moved into an apartment on Riverside Drive at West 113th Street, and into some rooms in a Barnard dormitory. Wherever we lived that summer, however, our day remained as nearly the same as possible under the circumstances. At each apartment, a Sister Vigilant called the others to rise and dress quickly, only now we formed our silent double lines to walk through the bright early morning light to the Cathedral for Morning Prayer and Mass. The Sisters living at Barnard were always waiting in

Sisters moving

formation at the corner of 116th Street and Broadway to fall
into step with the Riverside contingent as they came up the
hill. After the hour of prayer and worship at the Cathedral, we
would all go to the Riverside apartment for breakfast, the
living room somehow having been transformed into a
conventual refectory for twenty-four.

Summer school was in session at Charterhouse, and so after
breakfast the Sisters dispersed to various tasks, some to
Charterhouse to teach, others to college classes as students.
We always met for our meals at the Riverside apartment. In
the late afternoon we met again at the Cathedral for meditation
and Vespers. We had a little while back at our lodgings in the
evening for talking, sharing our thoughts and the events of our
day, before saying Compline together and retiring in the Great
Silence. Those few but treasured moments of sharing in such
a relaxed and simple way helped us to know each other better
and to be more helpful, understanding, and loving. We felt an
amazingly strong sense of oneness during this Diaspora. That
summer we had several Professions and the Clothing of at
least one Novice. These services took place in St. James'
Chapel in the Cathedral.

Meanwhile, the Convent renovations proceeded, as did the construction of the new School building on 114th Street. Bringing the three houses on West 113th Street together constituted the major problem, since the property is set on a hill between Broadway and Riverside Drive. Each of the structures has five stories and a basement. While the two east houses, 619 and 621, are level with each other, the west house, 623, is lower. The connections into it required three or four steps to each story. In order to accommodate the whole Community and guests in a chapel, the new Chapel on the third floor was designed to take the entire front of all three houses, with a free-standing altar connecting the guest part in 623 with the Sisters' part of Chapel in 619 and 621. The results were very satisfactory.

A plumbers' strike interrupted work on both Convent and School during the summer, even threatening the School's

opening date in September. Fortunately, however, the bathrooms were completed in time and school opened on schedule with special arrangements. Since the kitchen was not yet functional, meals were catered by Horn and Hardart. Classes continued calmly and efficiently in spite of the construction and disrup-

A gift to the Sisters from Madeleine L'Engle Franklin in memory of her mother

tion going on around us. At the same time, there was no disruption of the necessary ongoing demands of training the Sisters for their work of teaching. Thanks to the Deaconess Fund, which provided scholarships for Sisters, and to various incentive awards earned by Sisters themselves for outstanding academic work, our education continued. Where necessary, the School paid half the tuition for Sisters and the Community matched these funds.

In September the Convent was not finished, but Barnard needed its dormitory space again. Columbia University graciously agreed to postpone taking possession of Charterhouse since we badly needed these living quarters. The Community reorganized its temporary living arrangements once more: the Novices returned from Melrose and moved into the apartment on West 113th Street; the Professed Sisters moved into Charterhouse. We organized a Chapel in Charterhouse and resumed the recitation of Lauds, Vespers, and Compline, with a Noon Office replacing the Little Hours. All of our meals were served at Charterhouse, cooked on two hot plates and a small portable oven. There were two old refrigerators in the basement. At one point we were feeding thirty-five people from that little kitchen! It was during this time that we began washing dishes at the table together instead of taking them out to the kitchen for only a few Sisters or Novices to wash.

Up to this point, we had been using our small Office books, but we yearned to find our Vespers books. When the weather turned cold, we also needed our winter clothing, and so we made an expedition into the Cathedral crypt, climbing gingerly over all sorts of things, lifting down one box after another from the C.H.S. pile, looking for our names on the tags. Books and clothes were retrieved.

By Christmas, the new School Chapel and kitchen were finished. We began saying our Offices and celebrating the

Eucharist in the new School Chapel, and we cooked our Christmas dinner in the new kitchen and ate it in the new cafeteria.

In December Columbia took over Charterhouse, and the Sisters living there moved into the Paris Hotel on West End Avenue at 96th Street. The walk to school, sometimes on wet or snowy days, often took forty minutes. It was during this period that we rented a station wagon.

By the end of Lent 1967, the Convent was nearly ready for occupancy, but there was some problem about getting a certificate of occupancy. The Sisters so much needed to be back home again that finally Mother Ruth told us that we would be back in our home by Holy Week, with or without the certificate. We promised her that we would bake cookies for her in jail if she got arrested!

Actually the move was gradual, over a period of six weeks. Several Sisters moved in and occupied the upper floors while the ground floor was still open in places. Our favorite story from this experience is the burglar story. Hearing some noises during the night and suspecting a burglar, Sister Elise got up and tiptoed into the second floor of 623. She picked up the only weapon at hand, a heavy lamp, and stood behind the door poised and ready to hit the burglar on his head. Just in time, she recognized Sister Edith Margaret beyond the door! The entire family was thankfully settled in the new Convent for Holy Week.

In addition to creating a large enough Chapel, the renovation of St. Hilda's House had required the connecting of corridors, some division of large rooms on the top two floors into smaller rooms for each Sister to have her own sleeping quarters, and the provision of a Community dining room, kitchen, storage rooms, and laundry in the basement. It also required unified water, electricity, and heating systems. Two exits now led into the garden-to-be (the playground left by the school). An elevator now replaced the central staircase. Actually the work done by the construction company left much to be desired, especially in the way of plumbing, painting, and heating, but the Sisters now had a home furnished for reasonable comfort and almost enough space for the entire Community if the guest accommodations were also used. In the end, the School had expended over $280,000 on this renovation project.

After the remodelling of the three houses had been completed, and there were no more children to use the swings and slides in the playground, Mother Ruth said, "Let us make a garden!" The area behind 619 and 621 was of a good size, level, and well protected by a high wire fence. Why not give it a try? Whereupon the concrete floor of the backyard was broken up and taken away, to be replaced by load upon load of topsoil, delivered of necessity to the front door and carried through the house sack by sack. Here was now a splendid bed for flowers and lawn. The transformation of the yard of 623 took longer, since it was lower, and this project reached into the early 1970's. Nevertheless, the Sisters brought in stones by the truckload from Melrose, carrying them stone by stone through the house to the back, and constructed a rock garden between the two yards, with a wide patio of concrete for picnicking or parties, bordered with flower beds. Flagstones led from one level to the other.

Red roses planted to climb the back fence still survive. It has taken many years of experimenting, however, to discover what grows best in a city backyard that enjoys a modicum of direct sunlight. Spring bulbs are first followed by rhododendron and azaleas, which seem to be very much at home. A few hardy rose bushes struggle bravely through the summer, supplying admired blooms for cutting. From August on, when the sun goes further and further behind the tall buildings, we are grateful for the profusion of shade-loving but colorful impatiens. It is heart-warming to hear from time to time how much our neighbors, looking down from their apartment windows, enjoy our garden.

Looking back on this period and on the amount of endurance and perseverance it required, we are grateful for its blessings. Even the four Sisters who were in Peoria were made to feel a part of this experience through letters and their short visits home. Amid the general situation of dispersion, Sisters maintained a meaningful sense of continuity and unity, and the bonds formed among us by the long walks, the rendezvous for meals and for Services at the Cathedral, and the fellowship of the small family units living together will last a lifetime. Still, how happy and grateful we now were to be together under one roof!

The Sisters of the Community of the Holy Spirit in the garden

The Melrose sign

VII

Melrose

It quite soon became evident how much our growing school in New York City was demanding from the relatively small group of Sisters in terms of time, energy, and personal concern. A place must be provided to give them an occasional rest and change. Where would such a place be found? It was hoped to find, somewhere in the country, a property of sufficient acreage with at least one house upon it. Our method of locating such a place was twofold: we would consult agencies, and we would search directly for such a property and building for sale. The latter effort meant spending two or three days a week on the roads, accompanied by a young architect friend from Toronto who was keen about our need and well known to us. We chose to go north from the city, where there were many hamlets as well as larger towns and where the cost and distance from St. Hilda's and St. Hugh's would be within reasonable limits. This was in the summer of 1959.

The search led for the most part up through western Connecticut. A real estate agent from Danbury, a Mr. Murphy, became very interested. After showing us a number of places where the house was hotel size, or the acres too few, he escorted "the girls," as he had come to call us, to a farm near Millbrook, New York. Here was a very old and charming New England farmhouse—but small, an apple orchard, and a planting of Christmas trees that looked promising. We knew by now that whatever property we bought, it must in some way become self-supporting. There was also a small stream in front of the house that had been dammed up to make a fish pond. The owner told us he was in the habit of catching himself a fresh trout every morning for his breakfast. This place was clearly more appealing to some of the Sisters who saw it than to others. There were certainly "ifs," but time was running short, and a decision had to be made. We decided to go home and think about it.

A few days later some of us went back, taking Father Wylie, our Chaplain, with us to get his reaction. Once again Mr. Murphy led the way up Route 22, all of one hundred miles from New York. It was a beautiful day. Father Wylie seemed to like it all very much. The owner was looking very hopeful, but still something held us from giving the final yes. Sensing our hesitation, Mr. Murphy told us that he had one more place that had just been put on the market that we must see. It would be right on the way back, just a few minutes from Brewster, New York. So we followed him, a bit reluctantly, back down Route 22 about fifty miles, then over toward

Connecticut on what turned out to be Federal Hill Road, and finally up a long private driveway to the top of a hill. Here was a lovely two-story New England type house, a small amount of lawn, a few trees, and a superb view looking west over the rolling countryside toward the Hudson River Valley.

We were greeted by a Mr. Hoffman, who was very hospitable, showing us all over the house, then inviting us to sit out under the trees where we might have a glass of ginger ale and enjoy the view. This we did, and had some pleasant exchanges. The property, we learned, was actually owned by a Moroccan gentleman, who was out of the country at present. It covered eighty acres, much of which fell away from this site in steep, wooded slopes. To the east, Mr. Hoffman said, was a private golf course owned by a retired insurance magnate. On the southern slope up which we had driven was a small guest cottage, an old barn, a few apple trees, and at the bottom of the hill, by Federal Hill Road, was a smaller barnlike building, once used for sheep, we were told, and later for chickens.

Mr. Hoffman became even more friendly when he found out that we were Episcopalians. It seems he had known Bishop Bayne at a time when they were acolytes together, occasionally playing marbles behind the vestry. We told him of our school, and of our long search for a suitable place for rest times. This was beautiful, we agreed, but we must have a property that might be productive in some way. Here there was so little level ground in all the eighty acres. It was then that Mr. Hoffman suggested we go to see Dorothy Fields, the songwriter, who lived just across Federal Hill Road. Though she may not have yet put her place up for sale, Mr. Hoffman knew she wanted very much to sell and move back to the city. Her husband, whose name was Lahm, had died quite recently, and her two children were growing up. Her house was beautiful and the property had all sorts of possibilities.

This sounded good, and looked good as we drove by on the way home. Mr. Murphy, of course, must arrange for an appointment first. This he did with dispatch, and two afternoons later Mother Ruth and three Sisters were being welcomed by Mrs. Lahm into her very lovely house. We were enchanted. It was one of the pre-revolutionary houses that had been added on to many times. There was a large living room with French doors leading out onto a wide veranda, an equally large dining room, both looking out over the same rolling countryside we had admired from the house on the hill. This view was less spectacular, but rather more comfortable to live with. There was also a small library, and a wonderful big kitchen. Mrs. Lahm, after showing us the entire house, beautifully kept and well supplied with bedrooms and baths on the third floor as well as on the second, took us through all the grounds: lawns, flower border, cutting garden, tennis court, swimming pool and bathhouse, and beyond to the caretaker's cottage. Here, too, was a garage with room for two cars, tools of all kinds, and even a small greenhouse, a vegetable garden, and raspberry patch beyond. What riches!

After this, David Anderson, the caretaker, walked us all over the rest of the property—through woods, across a small stream that fed quite a nice pond, more woods, and finally out into open fields that lay to the west, 125 acres in all.

When we discussed price, it was clear that Mrs. Lahm felt generously toward us. To think that we might have had to pay approximately the same amount for the Millbrook property, less than half the size and twice as far from New York! This property was incomparably more suitable for our needs, and as it turned out, with far greater potential than anything else we had seen. There were no questions this time about the rightness, for we all knew in our hearts Whose hand it was that had led us here.

Even before the formal "closing" with Mrs. Lahm, word came to us that the Moroccan gentleman was going to sell his eighty acres across the road for a housing development. What would this do to our new property? With much courage and, perhaps, a sort of leap of faith, Mother Ruth made the Moroccan an offer. After many protestations about his deep attachment to this land and his imminent old age, he agreed to accept our offer with the proviso that he retain three acres on the southeast corner, by Federal Hill Road, and have the guest cottage moved down to it, thus giving him a home in which to retire. How could we say no to such a plea? So the agreement was signed and sealed. Within a very few months the little cottage had been moved, the three acres nicely landscaped, and the whole sold to a Brewster citizen and his wife. As for us, we were able to buy both properties, thanks to mortgages from three Toronto friends who required no interest on their loans.

First, these properties must be named. Mother Ruth thought to name the Lahm property "Lindisfarne," for the holy island off the coast of Northumbria, where in the 7th century St. Aidan had been the first bishop. Father West did not approve, because, he said, the Brewster people would soon be calling it Lindy's Farm, and that just would not do. Next choice was "Melrose." Inspired at the death of St. Aidan in 651, St. Cuthbert had gone from Lindisfarne to Melrose Abbey to take monastic vows. Later he returned to Lindisfarne, to become its bishop. Melrose was approved by everybody, Mrs. Lahm's house became St. Cuthbert's, and the Moroccan property Mother quickly called St. Aidan's.

Now we must look for ways to earn money at Melrose. One of Mother Ruth's ideas had been to develop a jam and jelly business, raising our own fruit. But then we heard about Christmas trees, how they grow themselves, require no care, and seedlings are provided at no charge by the Department of

Melrose

The first Chapel at Melrose

Agriculture. One does not even have to plow the land—just make a small hole in the ground with a mattock, slip the six inches of seedling into it, firm it with a foot, and move on to the next. We ordered about eleven thousand seedlings.

The closing had been in February. Mrs. Lahm's David Anderson saw us through the first few weeks until we could find a caretaker to replace him. For this purpose, and to oversee all that must be done to turn the Lahm house into a Convent, Sister Mary Christabel drove up to Melrose from her duties at St. Hilda's and St. Hugh's twice a week all through the spring. We now had a Melrose car. This was "Beulah, the Buick," an ancient convertible our friend Mr. Murphy had sold us for something like fifty dollars. We felt quite sporting driving about in Beulah. But in time her convertibility gave out, and her top could not in any way be raised. This meant carrying umbrellas on rainy days en route to the Brewster Shopping Center.

Father Howard Bingley, the Priest at St. Andrew's in Brewster, found us a caretaker. His name was Harvey Meyer, six and one-half feet tall, and all brawn. He had a hardworking little wife, and six small children.

As for the Convent, first the beautiful big living room was converted into a Chapel: a handsome dossal was made to order to hang on the west wall, covering the French doors; a local carpenter built a predilla for the altar, and sufficient choir stalls. Father West provided out of his treasures a many-colored frontal that would serve for all seasons, a cross, and a pair of antique gilt and chrome candlesticks. One of the Sisters designed and built a Sacrament house to go with the cross and candlesticks, which we are still using today in the new Chapel of the Holy Spirit.

One day in May, Harvey telephoned from Melrose to say that the Christmas trees had arrived—all eleven thousand of them. (We had hoped they might be sent one thousand at a time.) So a crew of Sisters, dressed in "ecclesiastical blue jeans," as Bishop Boynton called our summer habits, drove up from the city every afternoon after school to plant until sundown. That first afternoon, when the wind blew and the rain began to come down hard, Sister Mary Christabel quickly produced a number of old shower curtains that Mrs. Lahm had left behind, for raincoats. So, undaunted, the Sisters went to work with their mattocks. It must have been quite a sight, for before very long a row of cars had lined up along Federal Hill Road to see what was going on. Everybody helped with the planting, Harvey, Mrs. Meyer, the six children, even the janitor from Charterhouse joined in. In time all eleven thousand trees were safely tucked in, filling over two large fields.

Sister Mary Christabel, as Sister-in-Charge, spent all that first summer at Melrose, completing the furnishings (there was St. Aidan's House to do as well), looking after Sisters on rest, and the Harvey Meyer Family. Father Bingley had taken a real interest in Melrose, and came to celebrate Mass in our Chapel as often as possible. On Sundays the Sisters usually went to St. Andrew's in Brewster, and occasionally to St. James' Church in Danbury.

During the following winter Sister Mary Christabel continued her weekly trips to see that all was well. St. Aidan's House was rented to a teacher for the school months, a procedure which helped to defray some of the expenses. In addition to all the furnishings, we had bought a second hand Ford tractor, with mowers, so that Harvey could keep the several acres of lawn in proper shape. This he did very well. The cold weather told a different story. One mishap after the other made it increasingly clear that Harvey, alas, was not really equal to the job, and must be replaced. We also realized that it would be far better to have St. Cuthbert's lived in.

In the spring of 1961, a very capable young man, with much farming experience, no children, but a wife who would be able to help with the Convent housework, was engaged. A few weeks later four Sisters, with Sister Mary Monica in charge, were able to move up to Melrose to live. Three of these commuted on weekdays to their work in the city, while the fourth, the Sister bookkeeper, was able to do her work at St. Cuthbert's, and have supper ready in the evening for the others. Commuting left no time to develop a jam and jelly industry, but Donald Nelson, the new caretaker, kept us well supplied with fresh vegetables and fruit. He put the raspberry patch in shape, pruned, sprayed and cultivated the apple trees on St. Aidan's hillside, and raised annuals for the cutting garden in the little greenhouse. He also planted dwarf peach and plum trees, which bear fruit very quickly, so in time we had our own larder well stocked with canned fruits and vegetables, and often a surplus to take to the city.

More Christmas trees were planted in this year and the next. For this chore, Donald rented a mechanical planter to hitch to the Ford tractor. With two Sisters following behind to press the soil around each tender seedling, we were able to plant several thousand in a day. What a difference! In four or five years we began to sell a few. Then, for several years, we opened the fields in December on a "come and cut your own" basis. Families from near and far came with their children on weekends. On these days Donald kept shop in the fields from dawn until dark, his wife helping when possible, and we delivered food and hot drinks to keep them warm.

Early in the summer of 1961 Father Bingley retired, and moved away from Brewster. It was then we learned from the Rector of St. James in Danbury that his curate, Father Spear, was committed to a daily celebration of the Eucharist, and would welcome the opportunity to come to us. And so he did, for ten or twelve years, six days a week without fail, and often bringing one of his four small sons to be his acolyte. Father Spear's deep and dear devotion to our Lord was a source of blessing to all at Melrose. He also brought with him on Saturdays a young woman, Jean Morgan, who became the first Melrose Associate, and who has continued to come to our Saturday Mass through these twenty-five years.

Another enterprise that was begun in the summer of 1961, and continued for many years, was the summer camp for young children. A two-week session was held just before the opening of St. Hilda's and St. Hugh's summer school, and another in August after its closing. We did not attempt to compete with the usual summer camps for older children, with their horses to ride and boats to sail, though we often talked about it. But for the children of kindergarten age through about Grade Three, most of whom had spent their young lives in apartment houses without so much as a backyard to play in, we could offer all of the out-of-doors with its many wonders —sun and stars, birds, hikes in the woods, games, water play in a plastic pool, and the big pool for swimmers. There was for them also the splendid learning that comes from group living. These sessions were held in St. Aidan's House, and were run by two or three Sisters, with "counselors" from the upper school to help. The project proved to be a boon to a number of parents as well as for the children, and a much needed source of income for Melrose.

VIII

The Melrose School

In the fall of 1962 the Sisters began to think about the possibility of starting a school at Melrose. There were many small communities nearby in both Connecticut and New York which we might serve in this way. After all, educating children was our given work. That winter, though still commuting to the city, the Sisters visited every Episcopal parish Priest in the area, from Ridgefield, Connecticut, to Pawling, New York, to see what interest there might be in such a project. The Priests responded warmly. For many of the parents Episcopal Sisters were something new and strange. But by the end of the next summer quite a number of young mothers had become interested, though not quite ready for a commitment. Early in September 1963 these were invited to an open house to see St. Aidan's House, which would be the schoolhouse, and to meet Mother Ruth. There Mother Ruth could talk to them all about the education of young children and, too, about our vision and hopes for the Melrose School. Just a week later the School opened with a kindergarten of eight children.

Sister Jerolynn Mary, who was an experienced elementary school teacher, took on this challenge with care and love. Sister Virginia Mary (they were both Novices at the time) helped out with some vigorous singing and dancing. Little by little more children came. In the summer of 1964, after the Novices had returned to St. Hilda's House to make their Profession in First Vows, Sister Edith Margaret was sent up to teach Grade One, and to head the little School. At her suggestion, we spent many hours driving through various residential districts looking for children, putting a flyer in likely-looking mailboxes, and unabashedly peering at the contents of clotheslines. When a place looked promising, we rang the doorbell, hoping we might be let in to sell our particular wares.

One day during these beginning times, we received a call from Mr. C.V. Starr, our wealthy neighbor and owner of the private golf course next to St. Aidan's. Mr. Starr wanted our permission to have his men cut back the tops from a few of the old maple trees on our property that were hiding his view—the same view of the western hills that we had been enjoying so much. Permission granted, we were invited to drive through the road around his golf course "anytime," to see the naturalistic sculptures that were placed in very lovely settings. Some time later, he invited Mother Ruth, with several of the Sisters, to luncheon at his house, and this occasion was the beginning of a most happy and rewarding friendship.

The School grew. In 1966 the kindergarten was moved down to St. Cuthbert's House to make room for Grade Three. The sign that hung at the entrance to our drive read,

THE MELROSE ELEMENTARY SCHOOL

for Grade Three, we thought, must be our limit. But our parents were becoming increasingly enthusiastic, pressing us to go on. We did, adding a fourth grade, and then a fifth. By 1967 we knew we must think very seriously about building. The new St. Hilda's and St. Hugh's had been completed in 1966, and was now going strong. We took counsel with Mr. Starr, who soon came up with a plan. It seemed that Mr. Gordon Tweedy, Chairman of the Board of C.V. Starr Co., and Mrs. Tweedy were very keen to buy St. Aidan's House and its property. If we would sell, Mr. Starr would add to the Tweedy offer enough to bring the total amount to $200,000, giving us thereby a sizeable head start toward a fund for building. Further, to make the changeover more feasible for us, he would have his resident architect, Mrs. Park, convert the small barn on Federal Hill Road into an interim Convent. We would retain ownership of same, together with three acres around it. And since the Tweedys would like to be able to move into the house on the hill as soon as possible, Mr. Starr would make his guest house available to three Sisters while the barn was being prepared.

We looked at Mr. Starr's generous proposal with care. Although some of the Sisters, especially those who had spent much time in St. Aidan's House, were loath to see it go, we knew we could not refuse such an offer. After all, we had bought this property in the first place as a protection against subdivisions. This protection would now be secured, and we would be relieved of the cost of maintenance and upkeep of a large house, and more, we would receive more than twice what we had paid for it. So we accepted Mr. Starr's proposal, and within the year we were able to move into a new and smaller St. Aidan's House. At his request, it was painted a New England barn red. Then his gardeners appeared, planting trees and shrubs, and making a lawn all around the house. Inside, Mrs. Park's planning had provided for all our needs: Chapel, refectory, kitchen, laundry, a common room on the second floor and bedrooms and baths for at least five Sisters.

Now our greatest concern was the growing Melrose School. Kindergarten and five grades now filled the whole first floor of St. Cuthbert's, plus a bedroom on the second floor. In spite of these makeshift classrooms, we now had a real School. The grounds were ideal for games. There was sledding, too, in winter, kite-flying in the spring, and swimming later. The Sister who came in 1967 to head the School added several new dimensions, beginning with an art program. By 1970 the School was able to offer a full curriculum, a school newspaper called the *Skylark*, a well-attended Christmas Pageant, and a Children's Art Exhibit. Trips to the Katonah Art Gallery also helped to make the School better known in the wider community. We realized now that our School had an identity of its own; children, teachers, and parents together had become something bigger, a living thing that must be nourished and cared for. While this spiritual reality was most important, we still needed a building, and very badly.

Meanwhile we had had plans for a School and Convent, submitted by an architect, that did not seem to suit our tastes or our needs. Mr. Starr, who knew of our dilemma, suggested that we consult a San Francisco architect by the name of Burton Rockwell, who was at present teaching in the School of Architecture at the Massachusetts Institute of Technology. Mrs. Park knew his work well, and knew also that he had designed a number of schools in California. It was not long before Mr. Rockwell came to see us. He was enthusiastic about the project and the property. He made several trips to Melrose during the autumn of 1970, studying the whole landscape in detail, taking endless photographs of every view, of trees, stone walls, and existing buildings. We discussed our needs with him at length. The plans were to include classrooms for kindergarten and eight grades, a library with a fireplace, Mother Ruth insisted, a gym or multi-use area, a Convent, and a Chapel to be shared with the School. The plans were completed in the spring of 1971. When Mother Ruth had approved them, as did the Southeast Planning Board, all the parents were invited to a meeting. They turned out quite handsomely on an unpleasant, rainy night. Their interest and enthusiasm were heartwarming. Mother Ruth spoke to them about the proposed building, and what the Community had in mind for their children. Committees for a fund-raising campaign were set up then and there. Parents had expressed again and again their belief that this School had "something special" about it that could be found nowhere else. The Sisters thought to themselves. "May the Lord help us to nourish and serve this something!"

Nevertheless, the bulk of the financing came from St. Hilda's and St. Hugh's School in New York. The matter of funding the Melrose School building was brought to the attention of Mr. Hermann Place, Vice-Chairman of the Board of Trustees, with some trepidation, since payments for the New York School were not nearly finished. Mr. Place called a meeting of the Trustees forthwith. With a vast draft due on that new building, many had initial misgivings. Finally, realizing that the equity in the new Melrose building would belong to St. Hilda's and St. Hugh's, the full consent of the Board was granted.

And so, at last, ground was broken in September 1971 for the Melrose School. Bishop Donegan was there to conduct the ceremony; Mother Ruth was there with the same shovel she had used to break ground for the city School, which she now wielded with an experienced hand; and many Sisters and friends came up from New York to join all the excited Melrose children gathered around the site with their families.

Construction began the next day. You may imagine with what intense interest children and Sisters watched its progress. Little by little the long complex of one-story buildings we had seen sketched on paper became a concrete reality. Perhaps the most spectacular sight was when the huge beams, made of laminated hardwood, were hoisted by the long arm of a derrick, and dropped skillfully into position. These formed the framework of the structure, and remained for the most part exposed to view. They were beautiful. Classrooms were left unceiled, that is, with only the low-pitched roof overhead, giving a sense of space, freedom, and quiet. Both Chapel and kitchen were designed to be shared by Sisters and children, while the Convent wing stretched out beyond the Chapel toward the woods in quiet seclusion.

The natural materials of wood and stone were used inside and out wherever possible: stone fireplace and chimney in both libraries and in the Sisters' Common Room; and in the Chapel a huge stone, unearthed during the excavations, formed the base of the altar. The Chapel walls were of simple fir siding, a wood that becomes warm and mellow with age. The exterior is of unfinished California redwood which, after fifteen years of exposure to sun and shade, wind and rain, continues to change. It, too, seems to have a life of its own. Low stone walls in front of the School, with a bit of lawn in between, help the whole to nestle into the landscape. The high point of the complex is the bell tower. The idea of having a bell tower had been inspired by Mr. Starr.

The Melrose School from the front driveway

The Melrose Chapel

In September 1972, the Melrose School, now having kinder-garten and seven grades, moved into the new building with much rejoicing by all concerned. A few weeks later the Sisters were able to move, bag and baggage, into the new Convent. It was good to be all together again. On November 19th Bishop Donegan came out for the Blessing of Chapel, School, and Convent. It was a very heart-filled Thanksgiving that follow-ed soon after, with the first real feast out of the new kitchen.

Before these things came to pass, and to our great sorrow, our dear friend Mr. Starr had died quite suddenly. Knowing that he had looked forward to hearing "a peal of bells ring out over the valley"—his valley—the C.V. Starr Foundation made it possible to have a peal of eight bells cast for us at the White Chapel Bell Foundry in England. In the summer of 1973 Mother Ruth traveled to England and actually watched the bells being cast in the same foundry that had cast the bells of Big Ben, the "Oranges and Lemons" of St. Clement Danes, both in London, and the Liberty Bell of Philadelphia (which they have offered to re-cast, but to no avail).

The Bell Tower with bells installed

Sometime in October the bells arrived from England together with Mr. Bill Theobald who was sent to supervise their installation. Mr. Theobald had been with White Chapel for nearly forty years and knew his business well.

His first move was to send away the large crane our building contractor had brought in, as he thought, to hoist up the bells just as he had hoisted the structural beams. Instead a small truck carrying a winch with plenty of rope was driven in beside the tower. With this more primitive equipment each bell was lifted up most carefully and guided into its place by the skilled hands of Mr. Theobald. This was not the end of his labors. Once all was in order, he had the equally difficult task of introducing Sisters into the mysteries of bell ringing. The first thing we learned was that this required skill rather than muscle. A twelve or thirteen year old could do it.

Fortunately, before Mr. Theobald returned to England, he found through the Guild of North American Bell Ringers a young Englishman by the name of Roberts who lived not too far away and who was willing to come to Melrose once or twice a week to give instructions. There was great excitement about it at first, and Mr. Roberts had his hands more than full. Parents as well as Sisters and children wanted to "have a go" at ringing.

In time we learned that it was one thing to raise a bell and ring, say, the Angelus, but quite another to be one of a band of eight, each of whom must ring his own bell in exact and pre-arranged order with perfect precision. That is, change ringing. It demands hard work and a serious commitment. One by one our would-be ringers fell away, either for lack of time or lack of zeal. A few of the children were very apt, but they would soon be going off to high school. Some of the Sisters have stayed with it and done well, but never more than one or two at a time. It was the Guild of Bell Ringers that came to our rescue. Through them we learned of other groups around New England from various schools and churches who enjoyed going about to ring in other towers. Eventually we developed a regular Melrose band by advertising in the local

*Procession of the Participants in the Service of the Blessing of the Bells
with Bishop Allin, Mother Ruth, Bishop Donegan, Bishop Ramsey's
Chaplain, and Bishop Michael Ramsey*

papers. The Guild supplied us with the necessary tower captain. It was also through the Guild that our first instructor,
Mr. Roberts was able to obtain a band to ring for the coming
ceremony of Blessing the Bells.

This great event took place on the 31st of January, 1974.
Bishop Donegan, knowing that Dr. Michael Ramsey, the
Archbishop of Canterbury, would be in New York for a
meeting of bishops at this time, had invited him to come to
Melrose to bless our new English bells. You may imagine our
joy when we heard that Dr. Ramsey had accepted and was
really coming! All the Melrose world gathered together to be
present for this occasion. Chapel and gym, which served as a
large nave when the folding doors between were opened, were
filled to overflowing. Many more guests stood in the halls or
waited outdoors. Miraculously, it was like a summer day, and
no one seemed to mind, though the wait was long. An elegant

Dedication of the Bells

luncheon for twelve guests, that had been especially prepared by a school parent-restaurateur, was ready and waiting in St. Cuthbert's kitchen. At long last a motorcade came into the driveway, bearing the Archbishop and Mrs. Ramsey, Bishop Donegan, Canon West, our Warden, Chaplains, and last, but not least, our Presiding Bishop, the Most Reverend John Allin. Luncheon must be served first, while guests continued to wait in patience. Then all moved to the Chapel, and soon the ceremony began. After the prayers of dedication and blessing, and a homily in which he told us that the bells were "a sign that there are still a few good things that can come from England," the Archbishop climbed up into the bell tower to bless each bell by name—names that had been chosen by Bishop Donegan, Mother Ruth, Mother Mary Monica, and those most closely associated with Melrose, including Mr. Rockwell, the architect. As each bell was named it was rung once, telling forth its own particular tone. Quite unexpectedly, each ring was accompanied by a wolf-like howl from some-where down below. It came from Tobit, the old Newfound-land dog who had been a cherished companion of Sisters and children for the past ten years. Tobit had learned this art as a pup, when Sister Agnes used to ring the morning and evening Angelus on a large fire bell that hung outside of St. Cuthbert's Chapel. The bells for him must have brought back old times.

Tobit howled as the bells were rung

As the Archbishop went back down the narrow, steep stairs of the tower and returned to the Chapel, the crew of waiting ringers burst forth with a full and glorious peal. Canon West, master of ceremonies, led the procession out of Chapel and through the nave. Arriving at the doors, he turned to discover that Dr. Ramsey had been left far behind, for he had been stopped by the upturned faces of all those little children, some of whom must have thought this was God himself who talked to them so kindly.

The Melrose School quickly grew into the new building, much as a child grows into a too-large pair of new shoes. By 1973, the School was serving one hundred twenty children, from kindergarten through Grade Eight. This growth presented a fresh problem. The play area had been considerably diminished by the new school building. The remains of a tennis court, swings and slide were far from adequate for Seventh and Eighth Grade boys and girls. Mother Ruth sent word that Melrose must have a real playing field. Happily there was a large open field little more than a stone's throw from St. Cuthbert's House that had not been planted in

Christmas trees. Though at first glance it looked more suitable for sledding than for baseball, it had some advantages: it was nearby, it was invisible from Federal Hill Road, and it was easily accessible by car. We were told that it could be graded, and that, after grading, it would have excellent drainage—a most important asset for a playing field. So, in the summer of 1975 the work was begun, and by 1977 the Melrose School could boast of a full sized, beautifully turfed athletic field. In 1985, thanks to a grant from the Starr Foundation, we were able to add a changing house equipped with showers, which is especially appreciated by visiting teams.

In the early days of the School, education of all who came was tried, but it became evident with time that the School needed to define itself and clarify its purposes. The 1975 School brochure stated that the School would accept children who were average or above in mental ability. A few years later this was further limited to those above average. Children who needed "special education" would not be able to find either the facilities or the faculty they needed at Melrose.

Although financially the School has had to run to keep up with the bills, its intangible riches have been remarkable from the start. Chief among these has been the warm relationship among the faculty and pupils, a "family atmosphere" particularly noted by the evaluation committee which gave us our accreditation to the Middle States Association of Colleges and Schools in 1985. The School is now an integral part of the larger community, lending its athletic field and auditorium to a variety of local groups.

The Convent wing is next to the woods. A large company of squirrels, birds, and wildlife—deer, possum, raccoons, sometimes a fox or a polecat—share the property with the Sisters. The latter are keenly aware of the cycles of the animals' lives, and of the peculiar disposition of each species. The clear view

of the moon and constellations from the hill on which the
Sisters live give them a heightened awareness of sharing in an
immense and gloriously created world.

Not far from the Sisters' Chapel is a small stone structure
called the Columbarium, where the ashes of the departed
Sisters are interred. At this writing, there are four Sisters who
have entered the larger life and whose Requiem has been sung
in the Melrose Chapel.

*A
Columbarium
for the Sisters'
interment*

*Mother Ruth
and Canon West
at a recent St.
Augustine's
Day Celebration
at Melrose*

The power behind the work is, of course, that which emanates from the spiritual lives of the Sisters: the daily Offices, the regular times of meditation, scripture reading, and spiritual reading. Old churches and chapels are often noted for their "prayed-in" atmosphere; the new Melrose Chapel, its red cedar panelling still fragrant, seems to us and to visitors to have achieved this quality already.

The whole family with Canon West at Melrose

St. Cuthbert's Retreat House and Chapel

IX

St. Cuthbert's

From the very beginning of its life as the Community of the Holy Spirit, it had been apparent to Mother Ruth and to some of the Sisters that they had been called to retreat work as well as to the major pressing call to provide a Christian education to all the students who came to them. This call came first through the many invitations from dioceses throughout the United States to come and give retreats and quiet-days in their own local or diocesan facilities. Many more such invitations were given than the Sisters could accept because of their prior commitment to their own Schools, St. Hilda's and St. Hugh's School in New York City, and the Melrose School near Brewster, New York.

Whenever there was space or holiday time Associates and others were invited as guests to the city Convent, St. Hilda's House, either for a conducted retreat, or their own private retreat. When the Community bought property near Brewster in 1960, it was even then part of the vision of the Sisters that eventually a Retreat House would be made available to Associates and to others. This was not possible until 1972 when the new School building was ready for occupancy, and the Melrose School could move from the large white pre-revolutionary house they had used for a number of years, and which, before that, had been the Convent for the Sisters.

Restoration was begun on the house in 1973, when partitions were removed, thereby restoring the rooms to the beautiful proportion and space they had before their subdivisions into classroom space. Sister Lucia was appointed by Mother General Ruth to be the first Sister-in-Charge. In one of her first reports she observed: "Michael Ramsey, 100th Archbishop of Canterbury, blessed the House for Retreat work, naming it St. Cuthbert's House, on January 31st, 1974, and we opened with a goodly heritage: A House that had been prayed in, where loving people had cared for each other, and with the support of a praying community."

Sister Lucia lived in the house, seeking to discover its own character. In a later report she wrote: "I have begun to get acquainted with its inner moods; it is gentle, quiet, spacious and open to gracious living. It is a house where people have been happy, prayed and worshipped together, and where music, love and friendship have abounded. It has never been harmed by wrong use or wrong care during its past two hundred years as a family dwelling."

This background of loving tranquility was pervasive. All who have come since its opening as a Retreat and Guest House have mentioned that there is some feeling unique throughout the house, but most noticeable in the living, or common, room. The Sisters understand this. This large beautifully proportioned room, with windows on all four sides, was the Sisters' Chapel for the more than ten years the Sisters had lived in this house as their Convent. During all these years the Eucharist was celebrated daily in this room; the seven daily Offices were sung here by the Sisters in choir, and the walls were saturated with their personal prayers.

Later, when an interim Convent was made available for the Sisters, and this house was used for the School, their prayers and Chapel services added to the feeling that something was here "set apart." This spiritual undergirding is not missed by those who come as guests or for retreat; they at once are caught up in this holy quiet, reverence, and grace. Even though now St. Cuthbert's House has its own separate Chapel of the Holy Spirit, the Sisters are always happy when, as an occasional event, a visiting group will celebrate its own Eucharist in front of the fireplace. Somehow they feel that the house rejoices to hear the beloved words and to sense again the presence of the Blessed Sacrament. With this beginning and background, how could the Sisters' venture into retreat work fail?

The first guests were Archbishop Ramsey, attending clergy, and others who came for the blessing of the house and the eight change-ringing bells in the bell tower. Through the generosity of a school parent who owned a catering service, the Sisters were able to serve lunch to this large group, for the caterers brought the china, silver, and all else that was needed. Although the common rooms on the first floor were ready, and there was enough china and silver to serve twelve, overnight retreats could not yet be offered, the space for eight guests on the second floor not being ready. Nor had the house been as yet advertised as a Retreat House.

The first overnight retreatant was the Priest Associate, the Reverend Delos Wampler, in charge of Barry House, the Retreat Center for the Diocese of Albany. His blessing was an affirmation of the action taken in opening the house for this purpose. A guest from Illinois, now Father Steven Giovangelo, made his pre-ordination retreat at the house, establishing a pattern which many seminarians have followed. The first solo-Associate retreatants came from Florida, California, and Oklahoma. These too encouraged the Sisters in their preparation of the rooms and furnishings for groups. For the Sisters, and especially for the Sister-in-Charge, this was a year of listening to the wind of the Holy Spirit and attending to His opening of doors.

The house, from the beginning, had to pay its own way. Most of the work was done by the Sisters who also taught full-time in the Melrose School, and by Sister Lucia, who was also Sister Warden of the Associates. Solo-Associate retreatants could be cared for during the weekdays, but groups at present could be accommodated only on weekends. As bedrooms on the second floor had now been painted and furnished, the first flyer was sent out to 150 churches in New York and Connecticut. Previously, local church groups had brought their vestries for one-day meetings, and word-of-mouth from those who had been guests began to bring others.

Work was begun to restore the third-floor bedrooms. Gradually walls were repainted and furnishings provided. The house was given several dozen beautiful sheets, but they all had to be ironed; yet these served until three Associates from Dallas, Texas, arrived in a camper, bearing drip-dry sheets and pillow cases, bath and hand towels, and a set of stainless steel dinnerware. Often someone arrived at the doorstep with the gift of a blanket or a bedspread. Through S & H Green Trading Stamps, the Associates collected and sent several small pieces of electrical equipment and dishes for the kitchen which made it possible to work more efficiently. The house being now ready for group retreats, a one-page flyer was again sent out to area churches.

Among the early retreat groups was one of eight seminarians brought by the Archbishop of the Armenian Church; Priest Associate Father John Scott brought a group from the Church of St. Mary the Virgin, New York City; and Madeleine L'Engle Franklin gave the first of her many annual retreats here. When the first Associate Retreat was offered, Mother Elise conducting it, it established a pattern for silent classical retreats, which have become known for the quality of silence and the excellence of the addresses. The need for a separate Chapel for the Retreat House became obvious. Heretofore, the retreatants had worshipped with the Sisters in their Chapel, a practice loved by everyone; but the early hour of the Sisters'

A retreat in progress in the Chapel of the Holy Spirit, St. Cuthbert's Retreat House

services was not always best for those in retreat, and there also was needed a set-apart space for the giving of Retreat addresses, rather than in the common room. The New York architect, Robert Hutchins, designed a Chapel to conform in style with the architecture of the old pre-revolutionary house, which was so well executed that it is often believed to have been an adjoining carriage house now converted into a Chapel.

The Sisters, together with gifts from the Associates, made it possible to build this beautiful Chapel, so simple in its interior walls of oak panelling, floor-to-ceiling corner windows giving breathtaking views to the west, and yet providing for the worshippers a sense of enclosure. The first continued use of this Chapel was made by Father David of the Order of St. Francis, who made his long retreat with us. Two Associates made the gift of enough new Prayer Books for twenty-four retreatants in mind to use the Chapel. The large gold cross behind the altar was a memorial gift by an Associate, Beth Kostenbader, of Eugene, Oregon, in memory of her husband Ira, also an Associate. After the Chapel had already been in use for some time, it was blessed by our Warden, The Reverend Edward N. West, of the Cathedral Church of St. John the Divine in New York City, October 1980, Associates and other guests being present.

St. Aidan's House, the smaller house across the road from the School and St. Cuthbert's House, was opened as a second Retreat House in the late 1970's. During the years St. Cuthbert's House had been used for the School, this house served as the Sisters' Convent. Here again the Sisters set up their Chapel, celebrated the daily Eucharist, sang the Divine Office, and carried on their quiet lives of prayer. And so this old pre-revolutionary structure, which had originally been a chicken house, was also blessed. When the Sisters' own Convent was ready for occupancy, this house was gradually restored and

A Retreat Group

A Retreat Group having dinner

furnished as an auxiliary Retreat House, with bedroom space for eight, thus now providing space at Melrose for twenty-four retreatants during the months from April through November. Because of the great cost of heating this house, it is not opened during the four winter months.

By 1980 the character and use of the Retreat House had been established. Two Associate Retreats, with Sisters as meditation directors, were now annually scheduled, filled, and had waiting lists.   This was also true of the annual retreat

Madeleine L'Engle, Associate Retreat Conductor

Madeleine L'Engle gave here. Joyce Goodrich continued to bring her meditation groups five times a year for sessions of five to six days' duration. Repeating guests from the area churches were now finding it necessary to reserve space a year or more in advance. The Sisters served them with joy and friendship, and were rewarded with the friendship and loyalty of many of these guests. Associates and these new-found friends, as well as strangers who called "out of the blue," usually at the suggestion of a former guest, came for midweek times of prayer and meditation.

There were also, among these new friends and Associates who lived within driving distance, a number who now came to help in ways they could: in the library or in the garden. One Associate came regularly to gather up the soiled linen from the closing retreat, took it home with her, a long drive, and returned with it fresh and folded. Another was faithful in draining the water pipes at St. Aidan's and putting up storm windows at St. Cuthbert's. It was becoming a place where many felt at home, and where they wanted to be as often as possible, loving to be with the Sisters in Chapel and helping in whatever ways they could. Having come and seen what was needed, they returned, one with the gift of a KitchenAid dishwasher, another with books for the library. One lovely gift restored to the house was a set of five Bibles that had lived there from 1812 until 1920, when the last descendant of that original family moved. Once she called to see the old home, and shortly after returned with the Bibles, which she felt belonged in this particular house.

In addition to the reverence and prayers that had filled the house ever since the Sisters' first use of it, it had now become a haven where all kinds of people returned to find peace, quiet, prayer, and friendship. Other religious communities also booked space: the Franciscans held their long retreat here in 1981, and the Priors' Conference of the Order of the Holy Cross spent a week in 1982. All of this activity came to a standstill with the fire of April 22nd, 1982.

That morning, a Thursday, preparations were being made for the opening of the Associates' Retreat the following day. Workmen, laying a new roof, had only a couple of hours' work ahead of them to complete the job. But how suddenly the unexpected can happen! Perhaps the workmen did not associate the possible danger of the high wind and the torch used in sealing the edges of the roofing? By ten in the morning the wind and the flame had found each other. Two fire companies came and by a quarter past twelve the fire was out. But the whole third floor was now open to the heavens and one corner of the second floor lay exposed to wind and weather. Ancient hand-hewn timbers and beams, now charred, testified to the ancient character of the building. Great structural timbers had to be replaced. Severe water damage was everywhere except in the kitchen wing. Smoke damage was throughout.

Sister Lucia's first work, when permitted to enter the house by the firemen, was to look up the telephone numbers of those who were to arrive within the next twenty-four hours, many from long distances. Fortunately these records were in the undamaged kitchen wing. Eventually all retreatants were reached and stopped at various points on their way. Then, since the house was booked for every weekend ahead, these groups or individuals had to be called and their visits cancelled. Only then could the Sisters assess the damage and the work of restoration that lay ahead.

And yet there was a blessing in all of this. While the entire interior of the house had needed repainting, the Sisters had seen no way that this could be financed. And now the insurance would take care of this, together with the cleaning of the rugs! Insurance covered the reconstruction; it did not cover the financial loss of the use of the house for the months ahead. Nor did it provide for the building of a second stairway to the third floor, in the process of being built at the time of the fire, which was required to meet the existing fire code. Not knowing of these particular needs, Associates, groups, and individuals who had shared the house's hospitality answered them through their gifts and contributions. This spontaneous response made it possible to restructure the third floor, insulating the roof and installing three-track windows so it was very comfortable in both summer and winter, with attractive bedrooms, bath, and a common room for six people. Joyce Goodrich had been promised that she could bring her group back on October seventh. With everyone cooperating, the house was ready for them late that afternoon, the guests arriving as the painters were leaving.

After having been closed for five months, the house was again beautifully restored and freshly painted. The new third floor, filled with sunlight, is always a favorite spot. The previous pattern of life fell quickly back into place. The same church groups kept their same dates year after year, and they and the Sisters came to know and love each other, and to look forward to their time together again, remembering the favorite dishes and the preferred rooms of each one.

Our retreat program continues to expand. The Associates' Retreats always have long waiting lists, and more retreats of this kind, open to all, are now offered. Many more men participate and return year after year. Madeleine L'Engle continues to lead an annual retreat, and other well known directors and speakers have included The Reverend Canon Edward N. West, Dr. John Macquarrie of Oxford, England, Dr. Diogenes Allen of Princeton, Dr. Geoffrey Wainwright of Duke University, Father Wampler of Barry House, and Brother John Charles, S.S.F.

The Sisters are increasingly able to branch out, to give more weekend and summer time to actual retreat work. Many groups, including St. Luke's in the Village from New York City, specifically request that one of the Sisters lead the meditations or give the addresses. Several Sister-led retreats of a specific interest, as well as planned summer retreats, are scheduled regularly. Large groups come for a specific purpose and use the facilities of the School or enjoy picnic living outdoors. Youth groups, which the Sisters often lead in meditation, have been welcome from the beginning, and very often make "offerings" of such yard work as raking leaves in the fall or gathering broken branches for the fireplace in winter and spring.

The Community at Melrose feels that the size of the facility is just right—that its particular gift is with the intimacy and exchange that is possible with groups of twenty-four or less. There are other retreat houses and conference centers that especially designed for large groups.

We have made recent changes in procedure, however. For many years the names of the conductors of the retreats were not listed. The belief was the people should come for "retreat" and not for the name of the particular leader. Now, however, since the retreatants are most often coming from some distance, and since so many more retreats are being offered, it is felt that a choice of retreat should be given.

The retreat program previously had no special advertising except that of flyers and word-of-mouth from satisfied retreatants. Recently a one-page newsletter has been mailed out listing the retreats for the months ahead. A special page about the Retreat House, and those who come and go, is always included in the *Associates' Newsletter*, for the Associates from the very beginning have been very much its backbone support.

And the future? Sister Lucia retired as Sister-in-Charge in September 1983, in order to devote herself fulltime to the Associates for whom she has been Warden since 1970. The use of the house and its offerings will of course change as different Sisters are given charge and bring to the work their own gifts. As old friends continue to come, new ones will find their way to the house who will bring their own gifts and add to the continuing deep love, loyalty, and commitment. New faces will grace the house in their own individual ways. The house is good throughout, physically good, spiritually good, built as only those old New Englanders knew how to build for graciousness of living, and designed to take advantage of summer breezes, winter sunlight, and the far vistas of hills and wooded areas. Perhaps Archbishop Ramsey's "chair" will always be kept as a memorial of his visit, and no future guest will be invited to sit on it—in its fragile antiquity—and the antique rugs and paintings and drawings will become more beautiful through the years. We hope the African violets will always be blooming on the long window seat and that birds will be forever feeding outside this window, that guests will continue to remark about the good beds and the home-cooked meals for which St. Cuthbert's House has already become known, and that the fine books in the library will endure to nourish both those who browse and those who study.

The house in its setting has grown more and more beautiful over the years: the ancient sugar maples that line the ancient road, the evergreens accenting the autumn foliage, the pale pink rhododendron that blossom in July, the fields and the pond and the hidden streams—especially the one that sings behind St. Aidan's—all of these. Many more trails will be built and explored in the years ahead; and always there will be prayer and silence, friendship and laughter, love and listening.

X

The Associates

The Associates of the Community of the Holy Spirit are some one thousand men and women, youth, and Priests, who by a simple commitment bind themselves in prayer, to the Sisters and to each other under the inspiration and guidance of God the Holy Spirit, to living a disciplined life of prayer and sacrament, friendship and mutual support.

From the very beginning of the Community's life as a religious order dedicated to the Holy Spirit, the founder, Mother Ruth, had in mind a strong supporting group of lay persons and Priests living their normal lives in their parishes, but also reaching out to others in the power of the Holy Spirit. The revival of interest in the Holy Spirit and His activity was still in the future when Mother Ruth wrote this preamble to the Confraternity Rule:

"Jesus returned in the power of the Spirit" is a phrase we read with special meaning in this "power" age. So often we are unable to do the good things we would, yet the Spirit of Power needs naught but a free rein in us to inspire, empower, and to transform our lives.

"The Spirit of God has indwelt us since our Baptism, and we confirmed His indwelling power...through the laying-on of the Bishop's hands. Now we want to give Him all the freedom in which to work his powerful will.

"Men and women communicants and Priests of the Church who are aware of these needs and who desire this power, have sought from us a spiritual link and a Rule that will assist this their quest. The Rule of the Confraternity is accordingly offered to those devoted members of the Church who are like-minded."

This Rule was written in the very early 1950's, and by 1955 there were a number of persons undertaking the six month probation. The Rule stressed the keeping of the Prayer Book days of Feasts and Fasts, and the saying of the daily Prayer Book Offices. It asked for regular and frequent participation in the Holy Eucharist and Sacramental Confession, and in the making of a spiritual communion whenever unable to receive at the altar; daily meditation, personal prayer and the reading of Holy Scripture; and the regular use of retreats and quiet-days. One of the unique points of the Rule read: "Members must strive to become quiet centers of the power of the Holy Spirit in their homes and parishes, being content to be busier at prayer than at other good works." Many who undertook this Rule in 1955 and 1956 and are still living faithfully by it have been witnesses to its lifelong formation of channels through whom the Holy Spirit can move. While the Rule is undertaken for a three-year period, after a six-month probation, there is available to the Confratere as well a beautiful service for the remaking of the promises.

The Rule for Priest Associate was also offered in the early 1950's. This was a spiritual tie with the Community, one of mutual support through prayer and in other ways that opened one up. It was not a Rule of Life in itself. Priests desiring a Rule of Life with the Community undertook the Confraternity Rule or, when it was introduced in 1964, the Rule of St. Augustine's Chapter. Many Priests keep one or the other of these Rules, often keeping the St. Augustine's Rule with their wives.

The Fellowship Rule, also offered during these early years, is a spiritual tie with the Community which, through the prayers and devotional practices, forms one into the life and love of the Holy Spirit. It is mostly used by men and women who have many opportunities for spiritual growth, study, and service in their own parishes, and who feel drawn to community participation rather than to the need for further discipline in their own spiritual lives; or for those whose works and duties or neighborhoods make it impossible for them to practice regularly the use of the Sacraments. It has been found that one can grow just as holy under this Rule as under one asking more in the way of devotional practices. It has been the experience of the Community that there is a right Rule for every person, but that it should be a "given" Rule, not one that one writes for himself.

Since the Community has believed that a Rule should be "given," and chosen as given, with the understanding that temporary and slight alterations could be granted under special circumstances, there was felt the need for a Rule midway in discipline between the Confraternity and the Fellowship Rules;

thus the Rule of St. Augustine's Chapter was offered in 1964. The preamble to this Rule reads: "This Chapter exists to provide a Rule for men and women who desire to bring their lives under the inspiration and guidance of God the Holy Spirit, and to find that service which is perfect freedom." This Rule is often kept as a preliminary to the probation for the Confraternity Rule. It is also kept by many men and women who are active in parish life as well as full-time work or study. Also in 1964 the Rule for members of The Guild of the Holy Paraclete was made available to the youth of the Church. This is a simple Rule for those high school students who have the intention of forming a conscious and abiding sense of the Presence of God the Holy Spirit in their daily lives.

There is one Admission Service for these five Rules. It takes place at the altar and is administered by the Priest who receives the promises to keep the Rule while one is a member. The Priest blesses and bestows the medal which bears the symbol of the descending Dove within the seven-pointed star, symbolic of the seven covenanted gifts of the Holy Spirit, the manifold Gifts of Grace: the Spirit of Wisdom and Understanding, the Spirit of Counsel and Ghostly Strength, the Spirit of Knowledge and True Godliness, and the Spirit of Holy Fear. This well-beloved "charge" is given to each candidate:

"Seek to grow in the spirit of prayer and love.
Live not for the world but for God.
Regard not the wisdom of the world,
But pray for the wisdom that is from above.
Learn what it means to deny yourself,
And may the Lord be with you in your heart,
And fill you with all holy joy forever. Amen."

The Community of the Holy Spirit, with its dedication to education in its many different forms, was from its earliest days very much involved in the giving of quiet-days and retreats. Mother Ruth was the pioneer in this work, going into the dioceses of Kansas, Texas, Oregon, California, and other areas of the far west, at the invitation of the various bishops, as early as 1954 and 1955. She gave many quiet-days on these visitations, and Associates were received as a result of these spiritual days of renewal. Different Sisters also began to go into the various dioceses, often following up the work the Mother had begun, and drawing the Associates into corporate spiritual groups.

These small groups grew in numbers. Often the loving outreach of Associates drew others into the fellowship; sometimes the Church-sponsored quiet-days they offered, or the retreats given by Mother or one of the Sisters on their visitations, would awaken in other people the desire for a deeper life and the purpose to seek this through Community support and Rule. Convenors were appointed in many areas to plan retreats, admission services, special days of observance and fellowship, and the itineraries for Mother Ruth's or Sisters' visits. Bess Maxwell and Nancy Ireland in Dallas; Henrietta Haughland, Pat Lofstedt, Jeanne Priest, Billy Putnam, Betty Baty and Dorothy Carlisle in Washington State have been among the many wonderful women whose dedicated years of service in this work have touched the hearts and lives of many, many people. Hattie Irelan and Elizabeth Kostenbader in Oregon, Frances Reynolds in Florida, and Doreen Anderson Wood in Oklahoma have likewise given themselves with generosity and spirit to the Associates whom they held linked together in spirit. Priest Associates in local parishes often took on the responsibilities of a convenor when there were many Associates in their area, and served most faithfully, as they do still. Many convenors write and mail newsletters to those in their own areas as well as in neighboring dioceses where there is no strong local group.

Thus, the network of Associates has grown, spreading now across the entire country, and in so many areas has deepened in friendship, vision, and prayer. The very special days of Community —Whitsuntide and St. Augustine's Day—are celebrated in many places by Associate groups gathered in Eucharist and love, just as the local Associates met for so many years at St. Hilda's House on these two days of our Patronal Festival and anniversary of Foundation.

An Associate Group with Mother Elise

Mother Ruth was the first Warden of Associates, and her deeply insightful spiritual guidance and warm personal support went out in letter after letter to those who sought this special link of friendship. These were the letters one never threw away, but turned back to many times for courage, light, and inspiration. Mother also began *The Occasional Paper*, issued several times a year and containing her letter, Community announcements, and always a carefully chosen theological article, often by an outstanding theologian or one of the fine Priests who served as lecturers, preachers and teachers for the Community itself. These small magazines were beautifully printed and have been bound together in yearly volumes, each containing a wealth of great spiritual and theological reflection.

In 1964, Mother appointed Sister Elise as Warden of Associates. She continued Mother's ministry of lively and wonderful correspondence and began the bi-monthly *Newsletter* to Associates. While Mother Ruth continued to write and edit *The Occasional Paper*, Sister Elise wrote often about the Sisters' call to intercessory prayer and encouraged Associates to write and telephone their requests for the Sisters' prayers whenever they could be of help or service. Over the years the Sisters have come to know their extended family well through the needs and sorrows they have been allowed to share with them, and through the joys, renewals, and thanksgivings that have glorified God so often through this sharing and these prayers.

In August of 1970, when Sister Elise became Mistress of Novices, Sister Lucia succeeded her as Warden of Associates and she continues this guidance and support today. In her first newsletter, she wrote of her predecessors and her own hopes: "Mother Ruth, your first Warden, nurtured each of you so individually and spiritually that this in itself is a tremendous challenge. And Sister Elise, in her six years as your Warden, has built into your lives deep spiritual understandings, loyalties, and friendships, as the numbers of Associates have grown. My own role? Please support me with your prayers, trust, and friendship, in the hope that I may be able to continue in the fine tradition already established before me, and that together we may grow into channels through which His Holy Spirit can enlighten the hearts of mankind and bring us to our potential: Life with Christ in God."

An Associate Group with Sister Lucia

An Associate Group at Hood Canal, Washington with Mother Mary Christabel

Sister's personal correspondence and her newsletters have sounded again and again, throughout the years, this ultimate call, whether as Sisters or as lay Christian people: the call to grow more deeply "into Christ, in God." And always, the loving, strengthening reminder comes, the power of His Holy Spirit to accomplish this, of which we unaided are unable.

The ministry which has probably been most responsible for the growing numbers and deepening life of our Associates has been that of quiet-days and retreats. Mother Ruth traveled months each year in the early days, often using Churches where there were no retreat centers, but always making whatever place the retreat was held in a place transfigured and thereafter unforgotten. Other Sisters followed, each bringing her own gifts to the growing ministry, and many served in parish schools, Church vacation schools, and special workshops as the work expanded. But Mother's great love for the retreat work, and her awareness of its incalculable help to people in their spiritual journeys, brought to birth her vision of a Retreat Center where the Sisters could provide year-round opportunity for those times of growth and silence. St. Cuthbert's Retreat Center, sharing the property of Melrose, is now the answer to this dream, and Associates from all parts of the country come each year to the several Associates' Retreats. Often, too, they come simply to spend a few days of refreshment and reflection, joining the Sisters for fellowship and worship and being blessed by the great loveliness of God's world in this very special, beautiful location.

At the same time, the Sisters have continued to make yearly visitations to many places, especially Texas and Oklahoma and the far west, where the many vital Associate groups welcome them to lead retreats and quiet-days and to share their lives as Christians. The Sisters invariably return from these long weeks of ministry with a sense of having received such overwhelming inspiration and blessing that the vessel of their pouring-out seems to have been filled, refilled, and overflowing. The love that has thus grown between the Sisters and the Associates throughout the country witnesses continually to the way in which the Holy Spirit reaches each of us through the shared silence, the reflection, the quiet interpersonal warmth, and the experience of contemplation which retreat embraces.

In the years between Community visits, many Associate groups have begun holding quiet-days and retreats, always open to other people and sharing these wonderful opportunities with them. Often they are led by Priest Associates, who enable that beautiful balance of a "kept silence" and warm, hospitable relationships to form the context in which the Holy Spirit speaks so deeply.

It is impossible to overstate what the Associates mean to the Community. Their trust, their love, their generosity, and their constant prayers keep us faithful when it might be easier to slip. The breadth of their interests and their multifaceted work in the world—from artists to business people, retirees to students, lawyers to construction workers—has kept us continually aware of Christ's loving and transforming presence to the world through the faithful lives of His people. Our prayers for them are a privilege that is among our most fulfilling obligations, leading into that bond of mutual vision, faith in God, and Christian love that turns all life in this world into God's own joy.

Postscript

You have now read the story of the life's work made possible by the way in which the guidance and permission were given by the Holy Spirit of God and were accepted early in the lives of many of us. Those who could and would assist during that time were both blessings and inspirations having an unaccountable effect upon us and upon myriads of the young who were under our responsibility as well as those well on the way to adult life. After spending a total of forty-two years as an educator, let me say that this work is the most demanding as well as the most rewarding that can be imagined. Nevertheless sharing insights from the Holy Spirit and passing them on to those who would listen is of greater importance by far, however, than the best—the very best—formal education!

During a long life many different opportunities for service to others have been available to those who permit themselves to be aware of the nudging of the Spirit of God. So many things might have been different for us in our response to this interior word from the Holy Spirit of God.

When I graduated from High School in New York, in the presence of a number of my friends, one of them who also attended the same Church and who was graduating from the General Theological Seminary asked me to marry him. I had thought for some time before this request that I had been inspired by our Lord to give myself to Him in the Religious Life. This good Priest was willing to understand that the call of the Lord comes first. With Thomas à Kempis we decided to "Let this be thy aim and care, that God be with thee in everything thou doest."

Being blessed by many happy human friendships over the years, it has often been difficult to remain completely detached. But did not Peter and James and John who were such good friends see to it that they were yet able to keep themselves free to serve our Lord first as well as any who needed them individually. This has been a constant reminder and a blessing to us on the human side.

I can never forget that during my lifetime there have been many opportunities for loving-serving and with age one sees more clearly the times of opportunity as well as those of missed opportunity. I have tried earnestly in my dealings with the School's faculty, the graduates, children, parents, friends, and those who also felt a claim upon me to do and to be what God in His goodness has called me to do and to be. I am grateful indeed that I recognize not only my myriad blessings, but also the shortcomings of whatever kind that I must bring to Him for forgiveness and redress, knowing that all shall be well.

St Hilda's and St. Hugh's School

The Mystery of Christmas

mimed by the pupils of the school

The Cathedral Church of St. John the Divine
New York

Thursday, December 15, 1983, 2:00 & 4:00 p.m.

Appendix

The Christmas Pageant

THE PROPHECY

Comfort ye, comfort ye my people,
Saith your God,
Speak ye comfortably to Jerusalem
And cry unto her,
That her warfare is accomplished,
That her iniquity is pardoned,
For she hath received of the Lord's hand
Double for all her sins.
The voice of him that crieth in the wilderness,
Prepare ye the way of the Lord,

Make straight in the desert
A highway for our God.
Every valley shall be exalted,
And every mountain and hill shall be made low:
And the crooked shall be made straight
And the rough places plain:
And the glory of the Lord shall be revealed,
And all flesh shall see it together:
For the mouth of the Lord hath spoken it.

Behold, a virgin shall conceive and bear a son, and shall call
his name Immanuel—God with us.

ANNUNCIATION

And in the sixth month, the Angel Gabriel was sent from God
unto a city of Galilee, named Nazareth, to a virgin espoused to
a man whose name was Joseph of the house of David; and the
virgin's name was Mary.

And the Angel came in unto her, and said, "Hail, thou that art
highly favoured, the Lord is with thee. Blessed art thou
among women."

And when she saw him, she was troubled at his saying, and
cast in her mind what manner of salutation this should be.
And the Angel said unto her,

"Fear not, Mary, for thou has found favour with God. And
behold, thou shalt conceive in thy womb and bring forth a
son, and thou shalt call his name Jesus. He shall be great, and
shall be called the Son of the Highest and He shall reign over
the house of Jacob forever, and of His kingdom there shall be
no end."

Then said Mary unto the angel, "How shall this be, seeing I know not a man?" And the angel answered and said unto her,

"The Holy Ghost shall come upon thee and the power of the Highest shall overshadow thee: Therefore also that holy thing which shall be born of thee shall be called the Son of God.

And behold, thy cousin Elizabeth, she hath also conceived a son in her old age: and this is the sixth month with her, who was called barren.   For with God nothing shall be impossible."

And Mary said, "Behold the handmaid of the Lord! Be it unto me according to thy word."

THE VISITATION

And Mary arose in those days, and went into the hill country, with haste into the city of Judah: and entering into the house of Zacharias and saluted Elizabeth.

And it came to pass that, when Elizabeth heard the salutation of Mary, the babe leaped in her womb, and Elizabeth was filled with the Holy Ghost; and she spake out in a loud voice, and said,

"Blessed art thou among women and blessed is the fruit of thy womb. And whence is this to me, that the mother of my Lord should come to me? For, lo, as soon as the voice of thy salutation sounded in mine ears, the babe leaped in my womb for joy. And blessed is she that believed: for there shall be a performance of those things which were told her from the Lord."

And Mary said:

"My soul doth magnify the Lord, and my spirit hath rejoiced in God my Saviour.
For he hath regarded the lowliness of his handmaiden.
For behold, from henceforth all generations shall call me blessed.
For he that is mighty hath magnified me; and holy is his Name.
And his mercy is on them that fear him throughout all generations.
He hath showed strength with his arm; he hath scattered the proud in the imagination of their hearts.
He hath put down the mighty from their seat, and hath exalted the humble and meek.
He hath filled the hungry with good things; and the rich he hath sent empty away.
He remembering his mercy hath holpen his servant Israel; as he promised to our forefather, Abraham and his seed, for ever."

And Mary abode with her about three months, and returned to her own house.

THE ANGEL APPEARS TO JOSEPH
Then Joseph her husband, being a just man, and not willing to make her a public example, was minded to put her away privily.

But when he had thought on these things behold, the Angel of the Lord appeared unto him in a dream, saying, "Joseph, thou son of David, fear not to take unto thee Mary they wife: for that which is begotten in her is of the Holy Ghost. And she will bring forth a son, and thou shalt call His name JESUS: for He shall save His people from their sins."

Then Joseph being raised from sleep did as the Angel of the Lord had bidden him and took unto him his wife.

THE JOURNEY TO BETHLEHEM

And it came to pass in those days, that there went out a decree from Caesar Augustus, that all the world should be taxed.

And Joseph also went up from Galilee out of the city of Nazareth, into Judea, unto the city of David which is called Bethlehem: because he was of the house and lineage of David, to be taxed with Mary his espoused wife being great with child.

And so it was, that, while they were there, the days were accomplished that she should be delivered.

And she brought forth her first-born son, and wrapped him in swaddling clothes, and laid him in a manger; because there was no room for them in the inn.

THE REVELATION TO THE SHEPHERDS

And there were in the same country, shepherds abiding in the field, keeping watch over their flocks by night. And lo, the Angel of the Lord came upon them and the glory of God shone around them; and they were sore afraid.

And the Angel said unto them.
"Fear not: behold, I bring you good tidings of great joy, which shall be to all people. For unto you is born this day in

the city of David a Saviour which is Christ the Lord. And this shall be a sign unto you: ye shall find the babe wrapped in swaddling clothes, lying in a manger."

And suddenly there was with the Angel a multitude of the heavenly host praising God, and saying:

"Glory to God in the highest, and on earth peace, good will toward men."

And it came to pass, as the angels were going away from them into heaven, that the shepherds said one to another, "Let us now go even unto Bethlehem, and see this thing which is come to pass, which the lord hath made known unto us."

THE BIRTH OF CHRIST
Behold your God!
Behold, the Lord God will come with his strong hand.
He shall feed his flock like a shepherd:
He shall gather the lambs with his arm,
And carry them in his bosom
And shall gently lead those that are with young.

And the shepherds came with haste, and found Mary and Joseph, and the babe lying in a manger.

And when they had seen it they made known abroad the saying concerning the child. And all they that heard it wondered at those things which were told them by the shepherds.

And the shepherds returned, glorifying God for all the things which they had heard and seen, as it was told unto them.

But Mary kept all these things and pondered them in her heart.

THE PRESENTATION IN THE TEMPLE
And when the days of her purification according to the law of Moses were accomplished, they brought Him to Jerusalem, to present Him to the Lord; (as it is written in the law of the Lord): and to offer a sacrifice according to that which is said in the law of the Lord,—

"A pair of turtle doves or two young pigeons."

And behold, there was a man in Jerusalem, whose name was Simeon: and the same man was just and devout, waiting for the consolation of Israel, and the Holy Ghost was upon him. And it was revealed unto him by the Holy Ghost that he should not see death before he had seen the Lord's Christ. And he took Him up in his arms and blessed God and said . . .

"Lord, now lettest thou thy servant depart in peace, according to thy word. For mine eyes have seen thy salvation, Which thou hast prepared before the face of all people; To be a light to lighten the Gentiles, and to be the glory of thy people Israel."

And Joseph and His mother marvelled at these things which were spoken of Him. And Simeon blessed them and said unto Mary His mother, "Behold, this child is for the fall and rising again of many in Israel; and for a sign which shall be spoken against; (yea, a sword shall pierce through thine own soul, also), that the thoughts of many hearts may be revealed."

And there was one Anna, a prophetess, which departed not from the temple, but served God with fastings and prayers night and day.

And she coming in that instant gave thanks likewise unto the Lord and spake of Him to all that looked for the redemption of Jerusalem.

THE COURT OF HEROD

Now when Jesus was born in Bethlehem of Judea in the days of Herod the King, behold, there came wise men from the east to Jerusalem, saying, "Where is he that is born King of the Jews? For we have seen His star in the east and have come to worship Him."

When Herod the King heard these things he was troubled. And when he had privily called the wise men, he inquired of them diligently what time the star appeared. And he sent them to Bethlehem and said, "Go and search diligently for the young child; and when ye have found him, bring me word again, that I may come and worship Him also."

When they heard the King, they departed.

THE VISIT OF THE WISE MEN

And lo, the star which they saw in the east, went before them, till it came and stood over where the young child was. When they saw the star, they rejoiced with exceeding great joy.

And when they were come into the house they saw the young child with Mary His mother, and fell down and worshipped Him.

ISAIAH

The people that walked in darkness have seen a great light: they that dwell in the land of the shadow of death, upon them hath the light shined.

For unto us a child is born, unto us a son is given: and the government shall be upon his shoulder: and his name shall be called Wonderful, Counsellor, the Mighty God, the Everlasting Father, the Prince of Peace.

Praise be to God who so loved the world that He sent His only begotten Son, that whoso believeth on Him should not perish, but have everlasting life. As our Saviour Christ hath commanded and taught us, we are bold to say:

ALL:
Our Father which art in heaven,
Hallowed be thy name.
Thy kingdom come.
Thy will be done in earth, as it is in heaven.
Give us this day our daily bread.
And forgive us our debts, as we forgive our debtors.
And lead us not into temptation, but deliver us from evil:
For thine is the kingdom, and the power, and the glory, for ever. Amen.

Cast of Mimers

ISAIAH   Bailey Franklin
READER   Alicia Galanter
SAINT MARY   Cecily Van Praagh
SAINT JOSEPH   Christian Avignone
GABRIEL   Mary Rakic
ST. MARY'S HANDMAIDENS   Serena Canin, Jennifer Corsun, Alexandra Hague, D'Arcy Johnson, Christine Lulejian, Allison Nurse, Ameeta Persaud, Denise Redman, Myoshin Thurman, Joanne Urena
SAINT ELIZABETH   Katherine Mavrovouniotis
INNKEEPER   Madeline Tsingopoulos
GUESTS AT THE INN: Jessica Avignone, Melissa Burkhart, Catherine Bushell, Vanessa Domingo, Lisa Kavanaugh, Ariana Krawitz, Wing-Man Lau, Catherine Luttinger, Kelly Madden, Hilary Redmon, Elizabeth Tesla
SHEPHERDS: Zoe Brugger, Alexander Coyle, Michelle Galanter, Seungno Hong, Natasha Joseph, Jason Li, Joelle Sprauve, Ingrid Varona, Brooke Walker
THE CHRIST CHILD   Emily Brown Wilson (2 p.m.)
Joshua Benjamin Mason (4 p.m.)
ANGELS: Alisa Aydin, Gabrielle Antoniadis, Chantal Avignone, Joan Corcoran, Katharine Derosier, Laura Freseman, Jennifer Leach, Martha Lesemann, Lisa Mitchell, Liza Schwartz
HIGH PRIEST   Charles Fairweather
ACOLYTES: Evan Jahn, Erik-Peter Mortensen, Jude Reveley, Giles Van Praagh
SIMEON   Christopher Jones
ANNA   Katherine Feller
TEMPLE DANCERS: Meredith Berlin, Nicole Di Iorio, Gabrielle Galanter, Helen Rakic
HEROD   Brian Stokes
CUP-BEARER   Elisabeth Tomere
MESSENGER   Catherine Milenkovitch
ROMAN CONSUL   Anthony Pappas
CAPTAIN   Charles Jones
SOLDIERS: Whitney Balliett, Jr., Craig Cabanis, Robert Fellvinci, Richard Nurse, Ian Van Praagh, Christopher Wilson
KINGS: Lucian Estevez, Kevin Tung, Vincent Nemes
KINGS' PAGES: Evelyn Finley, Jessie Howard, Elisabeth Matthew, Kristin Michaels, Wayne Silcott, Aline Sun, Thomas Verdell, Judy Vincent, Daniel Young
CANDLE BEARERS: Amira Grant, Holly Lynch, Nicole Pappas

The Mystery of Christmas

PROLOGUE: THE PROPHECY OF ISAIAH
The God of Christians is the God of promise, the God of hope. His word, spoken by the prophets, quickens the hope of the coming of a Deliverer of his people, a Messiah for all people. Iasiah proclaims this promise.

I.   THE ANNUNCIATION TO THE VIRGIN MARY
The promise of God is to be fulfilled in the body of a peasant girl who with her whole heart gives her consent to bear the Lord Christ. The human YES of Mary prepares the way for the Incarnation, the enfleshment of God.

II.   THE VISITATION OF MARY TO HER COUSIN ELIZABETH
The joy of Mary is the song of Mary which she sings in the presence of Elizabeth. The song of Mary is the song of the Church which she pesonifies. Her Magnificat praises the divine revolution, which breaks out when there is a human YES to God's call.

III.   THE ANGEL APPEARS TO JOSEPH
God's Messenger comes to Joseph to allay the natural suspicions of this just man, and to announce to him that the Christ of God will be entrusted to his fatherly care.

IV.   THE JOURNEY TO BETHLEHEM
Mary and Joseph go to Bethlehem because their taxes are due. They are turned away from the inn in the first rejection of Him who is despised and rejected of men. Is there ever room for Christ to be born? Do you have room?

V.   THE REVELATION TO THE SHEPHERDS
It is Cold out there, and there may be wolves. Shepherds are not wise men, but again to the humble and meek comes a breakthrough of cosmic glory, and a word from the Lord to come - to a stable. What a strange God - shepherds - stable - Saviour!

VI.   THE BIRTH OF CHRIST
Jesus the Christ is born in a stable, a place of beasts with the stench of beasts. Such is the humility of God! And He who was born in a stable died on a cross; the manger is his cross at birth - the paradox of glory!

VII. THE PRESENTATION IN THE TEMPLE

Jesus is a Jew, a circumcised son of David, in obedience to the law of Moses presented in the Temple. But old Simeon sees that this Jewish child is born for all mankind, "a light to lighten the Gentiles." His Nunc Dimittis becomes the song of the Church of all the ages and all the races.

VIII. THE COURT OF HEROD

Here is the place of power, of the clash of cymbals and the flash of arms. The Wise Men come to this proud palace deceived by human wisdom. They must go to the stable to find the hiddenness of God, who does not show his glory in the strength of power, but in the power of love.

IX. THE VISIT OF THE WISE MEN

Glorious fragrant vision of strangers from the East, of gold, incense, and myrrh! Magi from afar, astrologers perhaps, give up their gifts, lay down their arts, before the crib of Christ. More is here than just the mystic East. It represents the savingness of Christ for us and for those unknown.

The end of the mystery here portrayed in pageant, its tableau, is a sign of the fulfillment of the promise and the hope we have in Christ. He who was born for us, and died for us, was raised from the dead, and given to us that in him on earth we may have peace, and in the end with all men and all things, be filled with the fullness of God.

The Presentation of Gifts by the Children of the School after which an offering will be received. The congregation should remain seated until all the children have presented their gifts.

The Pageant will close with "O Come, all ye Faithful."
Hymn 12, verses 1, 2, 3, 6.

Music

Advent Responsory	Palestrina
O Come, O Come Emmanuel	Adapted from Plainsong
Gabriel's Message	Basque Carol
Of the Father's Love Begotten	13th Century Plainsong
I Sing of a Maiden	Martin Shaw
Magnificat	Plainsong with Fauxbourdon
The Cherry Tree Carol	Old English
To Us is Born Emmanuel	Praetorius
Let All Mortal Flesh	G. Holst
Gloria in Excelsis	Willilam Toole
Psallite	Praetorius
The Christmas Hymn	17th Century Carol
Mi Chomocho	Salomone Rossi
Nunc Dimittis	William Tolle
Orientis Partibus	Medieval
Personent Hodie	14th Century German
Salve, Agnus Dei	from "The Play of Herod"

Production Staff

STAGE DIRECTOR	Shirlie Verrill Harrison
PRODUCTION MANAGER	Mother Mary Christabel, CHS
MUSIC DIRECTOR	Richard McCoy
TECHNICAL DIRECTOR	Jennifer Corcoran
STAGE MANAGERS	Kimberly Joyce
	Robyn Roberts
	Johanne Troemel

MUSIC ASSISTANTS AND INSTRUMENTATLISTS: Sister Regina, CHS, Sister Helena Marie, CHS, Novice Cecily, CHS

COSTUMES	Sister Dominca, CHS
MAKE-UP	Sister Penelope Mary, CHS
ORGAN	Paul Halley
CHOREGRAPHY	Diana Nicholson, Xenia Rakic
DRILLMASTER	Francis Sheehan
DRUMMER	Theodore Antoniadis

TECHNICAL CREW Theodore Antoniadis, Bruce Browning, Jeremy Hill, Mary Kieronski, Jean Kim, Alexander Krengel, Samuel Kretschmer, Andrew Milenkovitch, Christine Munzer, Salim Parmar, Adam Rafferty, Ramsey Shiber.

Special thanks to the Art Department and to the many parents and faculty who have so generously given time and materials to this production. And our gratitude to the Cathedral Church of St. John the Divine for continuing to provide us with the time and space we need.

Mother Ruth with Jonathan at her desk in the school